ST PAUL'S CATHEDRAL

The New Bell's Cathedral Guides
ST PAUL'S CATHEDRAL

PETER BURMAN

PHOTOGRAPHY BY MALCOLM CROWTHERS

BELL & HYMAN

First published in Great Britain by
Bell & Hyman, an imprint of Unwin
Hyman Limited 1987

UNWIN HYMAN
Denmark House, 37–39 Queen Elizabeth Street
London SE1 2QB

and 40 Museum Street, London WC1A 1LU

ALLEN & UNWIN Australia Pty Ltd
8 Napier Street, North Sydney, NSW 2060, Australia

ALLEN & UNWIN New Zealand Ltd with the Port Nicholson Press
60 Cambridge Terrace, Wellington, New Zealand

ISBN 0–7135–2616–5 (cased)
      0–7135–2617–3 (limp)

British Library Cataloguing in Publication Data
Burman, Peter
    St. Paul's Cathedral. — (The new Bell's cathedral
    guides)
    1. Wren, Sir Christopher, 1632–1723   2. St. Paul's
    Cathedral, London — Guide-books 3. London
    (England) — Churches
    I. Title
    914.21'2   DA687.S14

Designed by Janet Tanner
Typeset by Latimer Trend & Company Ltd
Printed and bound in Great Britain
at the University Press, Cambridge

CONTENTS

Chapter One

THE EARLY HISTORY OF THE SITE AND THE PREDECESSORS OF THE PRESENT CATHEDRAL

CHRISTIANITY WAS well established in Britain in Roman times: the martyrdom of St Alban, the first British martyr, is thought to have taken place either in *c.* 254 under the Emperor Decius or in *c.* 209 under the Emperor Septimius Severus. British bishops are known to have taken part in various Councils of the early Church, and a Bishop of London, Restitutus by name, is given as one of the three British bishops present at the Council of Arles in 314. If there was a Bishop of London in the early fourth century, it is reasonable to assume that there was also a cathedral, since by definition a cathedral is a church which contains the 'cathedra' or official seat of the bishop.

In *Parentalia*, the writings collected by his son, Wren suggests that the first two cathedrals were built on the site of the Praetorian Camp. According to him, the first was demolished under Diocletian; the second rebuilt on the same foundations under Constantine but destroyed by Saxons some time later. When digging the foundations for the north-east corner of the new St Paul's, Wren came across evidence of a Roman pottery 'where all the Pot-earth had been robb'd by the Potters of old Time: Here were discovered Quantities of Urns, broken

Vessels, and Pottery-ware of divers Sorts and Shapes'; and there were also, in other parts of the site, 'Graves of several Ages and Fashions in strata, or Layers of Earth one above another, particularly at the North-side of Paul's [which] manifestly shew'd a great Antiquity from the British and Roman Times . . .'. Subsequent excavations to the north of St Paul's have also exposed Roman burials, which suggests that this area was a cemetery at least in the first and second centuries.

The first cathedral of London on this site, known to be dedicated to St Paul, was founded in 604 by Mellitus, one of a second group of missionaries sent over to England by Pope Gregory the Great. (The first group, led by Augustine, settled at Canterbury in 596–7, where Augustine became Archbishop.) If the earlier cathedrals had not been dedicated to St Paul, this would then have seemed an appropriate choice: for the faith of Christianity was being brought to the Saxons, as it had been to the Gentiles by St Paul, and—since dedications to Peter and Paul are often linked with one another—the dedication to St Paul would also have been a graceful tribute to Pope Gregory, whose papal basilica was St Peter's in Rome.

Unfortunately there is no evidence for the shape, dimensions, siting or appearance of the cathedral founded by Mellitus, which would certainly have been one of the most striking buildings in Saxon London, without rivals until the royal move to Westminster and the founding of Westminster Abbey. Some idea of what it may have looked like can be gained from contemporary buildings. At St Bride's, Fleet Street, for example, archaeological investigation has shown that there was an early Saxon church with an eastern apse. Similarly All Hallows Barking, near the Tower of London, has a surviving monumental arch, perhaps of the eighth century, and an original north-west corner extensively re-uses Roman tiles.

All Hallows also provides a link with St Erkenwald, who became Bishop of London in c. 675 and was a vigorous proselytizer of the surrounding countryside. He founded an abbey at Chertsey and another at Barking, where his sister was installed as Abbess, and where he died. Even in Saxon times it was advantageous to own property in the City of London, so All Hallows 'Barking Church' belonged to Barking Abbey.

This cathedral was occasionally used for the burial of Saxon royalty. Sebba (d. 695) and Ethelred, called 'the Unready'

(d. 1016) were buried there—their remains survived the fire of 1087 and were later provided with caskets which is how they appear in Hollar's engraving. In 1023 King Cnut participated in a ceremony to transfer the remains of St Alphege, a former Archbishop of Canterbury martyred in Greenwich in 1012, to Canterbury Cathedral. This decision undoubtedly deprived St Paul's of a considerable financial asset, for relics and their associated shrines, devotions and miracles were a great attraction to pilgrims throughout the Middle Ages, and consequently brought both wealth and prestige to those cathedrals and greater churches fortunate enough to possess them.

The destruction of the Saxon cathedral and the foundation of its Romanesque successor are described by John Stow in his *Survey of London*, 1598. 'In the year 1087, this church of St. Paul's was burnt with fire, and therewith the most part of the city; which fire began at the entry of the west gate, and consumed the east gate. Mauricius [Maurice] the bishop began therefore the foundation of a new church of St. Paul's, a work that men of that time judged would never have been finished, it was to them so wonderful for length and breadth; and also the same was built upon arches (or vaults) of stone, for defence of fire, which was a manner of work before that time unknown to the people of this nation, and then brought in by the French; and the stone was fetched from Caen in Normandy.'

There is some controversy as to whether the old foundations were re-used for the Romanesque cathedral. Stow specifically says that Bishop Maurice 'repaired not the old church, as some have supposed, but began the foundation of a new work'; whereas *Parentalia* gives Wren's opinion 'that though several Times the Fabrick had been ruin'd, yet that the Foundations might remain, as originally they were laid, was upon his observing, that they consisted of nothing but Kentish-rubble-stone, artfully work'd, and consolidated with exceeding hard Mortar, in the Roman Manner, much excelling what he found in the Superstructure'.

Although Maurice, who started the rebuilding work, was Bishop of London for another twenty years after the fire of 1087, he was only able to see the foundations and the laying out of his large new cathedral. His successor, Richard de Belmeis, did (according to Stow) 'wonderfully well advance the work of the said church, purchasing the large streets and lanes round about, wherein were wont to dwell many lay people, which ground he began to compass about with a strong wall of stone and gates'. Henry I granted him 'so much of the moat (or wall) of the castle, on the Thames side, to the south, as should be needful to make the said wall of the church, and so much as should suffice to make a wall without the way on the north side'. The 'castle' was probably Baynard's Castle, one of William I's western defences of the City; and it appears that an ancient stream flowed across what is now Paternoster Square, to the north of St Paul's, which would have had to be diverted or channelled to allow the building of the north precinct wall.

In a St Paul's cathedral document of *c.* 1138–50 Andrew the Mason (or 'Cementarius') appears as a witness; he may have been the designer, or at least one of the chief artificers, of the great Romanesque nave which was then in course of erection. Apparently there had been another serious fire in 1135, which again delayed the work, and the construction of the immensely long twelve-bay nave may have extended well into the third or fourth quarter of the twelfth century. The choir at any rate seems to have been completed by 1148, for on 14 November the relics of St Erkenwald were translated from their previous resting place in the crypt to a position in the apse, behind the high altar and close to the tomb of Bishop Mellitus. An inventory of 1245 describes this twelfth-century shrine as being adorned with images, encrusted with one hundred and thirty precious stones, and finished with figures of angels at either end. Such shrines still survive in certain of the Romanesque churches of Cologne, for example, but nothing on this scale survives in England to show the spectacular virtuosity and sheer splendour of contemporary shrines and the metal-workers' art.

The Romanesque church as completed consisted of a choir raised over a crypt at the east end, apsidal or semi-circular in its termination, probably with an ambulatory or processional passageway and radiating chapels. West of the choir was the crossing space, over which a noble lantern tower was to rise in the early thirteenth century, and the crossing space was the meeting point of deep north and south transepts; west of the crossing space began the twelve-bay nave, with north and south aisles divided from the nave by arcades with noble piers with clustered columns like those at Peterborough Cathedral. Attached to the south side of the nave at the west was the aisled, apsidal parish church of St Gregory, entered by doorways from the south. Stow says that 'at either corner of this west end is, also of ancient building, a strong tower of stone, made for bell towers'. These towers were outside the line of the aisles, and that on the south side interrupted the nave space of St Gregory's church. They appear in Hollar's plan, and also in his illustrations, but in his representations of them they are naturally shown clothed in Inigo Jones's stone cladding (or perhaps total rebuilding) of the 1630s and they look, in any case, surprisingly slender for Romanesque towers.

If we can be less certain about the towers, and if the appearance of the Romanesque eastern arm of the building is lost to us through later rebuilding in the Gothic style, we can at least enjoy to the full the appearance of the twelfth-century nave looking east in Hollar's engraving. This appears to have been taken from a viewpoint at the extreme west end. The piers are cruciform in plan, with clusters of attached columns supporting one inner and two outer orders of arches forming the arcades. Between each bay a similar cluster of vaulting shafts rises from the base of the piers to the vault. The triforium consists of wide single arches with three orders of attached columns; the clerestory windows are large single openings, and appear round-headed. In the aisles can just be seen, under the windows, blank arcading articulating the lower parts of the walls, also with round-headed arches. Over both nave and aisles (and no doubt transepts) are rib vaults, as at Durham. The effect is a noble one, even from the engraving, and it must have been one of the most impressive buildings in the whole country. Perhaps only Durham, Ely, Norwich, Peterborough and Winchester (the latter before its later gothicization) could have been mentioned in the same breath as being amongst our greatest Romanesque churches.

There seems to have been no sharp or sudden break between the Romanesque work and the early Gothic period. As we have seen, the work of building the nave and transepts went on for many decades; and G H Cook dates the clerestory stage as being of *c*. 1200 or soon after, pointing out that the openings in each clerestory bay are flanked by pointed blank arcading (just visible in the Hollar engraving) and are therefore 'the earliest piece of gothic architecture in old St. Paul's'. The construction of the high vaults obviously followed on from this phase, and the crossing piers were completed with pointed arches whereas if they had been built much more quickly they would no doubt have been rounded.

The next phase of work is succinctly given by Stow: 'The steeple of this church was built and finished in the year 1222; the cross on the said steeple fell down, and a new was set up in the year 1314. The new work of Paul's (so called) at the east end above the choir, was begun in the year 1251. Henry Lacy, Earl of Lincoln, Constable of Chester, and *custos* of England, in his time was a great benefactor to this work, and was there buried in the year 1310. Also Ralph Baldock, Bishop of London, in his lifetime gave two hundred marks to the building of the said new work, and left much by his testament towards the finishing thereof: he deceased in the year 1313, and was buried in the Lady Chapel. Also the new work of Paules, to wit, the cross aisles, were begun to be new built in the year 1256.'

Expanding somewhat on the information Stow gives us, we can look again at Hollar and see that the central tower or steeple consisted of two stages, each having three glazed lancet openings on all four sides. The lower lancets were immensely tall, perhaps about 60 feet (20 metres) in height, and the combined effect of the two tiers of openings must have been to flood the crossing space with light. Obviously this cannot have been a tower suitable for the hanging and ringing of bells, so (like Chichester and Salisbury, of which the former survives) St Paul's had a separate spired bell-tower in the south-east corner of St Paul's churchyard. At Ashwell church in Hertfordshire is an incised graffito drawing perhaps of the fourteenth century, which shows both the separate bell tower and also the exceptionally lofty spire over the central tower. This spire, which was of virtuoso timberwork covered with lead, was considerably taller than the stone spire of Salisbury Cathedral. G H Cook suggests that 'John the Carpenter', who between 1229 and 1241 was granted a lease of certain stone-built houses belonging to the Dean and Chapter of St Paul's, outside their churchyard to the north (i.e. where Paternoster Square is today), might have been the carpenter responsible for the framework of the spire.

This central spire was destroyed in 1561. In Stow's words: 'In the year 1561, the 4th of June, betwixt the hours of three and four of the clock in the afternoon, the great spire of the steeple of St. Paule's church was struck by lightning, which brake forth (as it seemed) two or three yards beneath the foot of the cross; and from thence it went downward the spire to the battlements, stonework, and bells, so furiously, that within the space of four hours the same steeple, with all the roofs of the church, were consumed, to the great sorrow and perpetual remembrance of the beholders.' Queen Elizabeth I wrote at once to the Lord Mayor, urging him to take speedy action for the repair of the roofs and steeple; and she 'did presently give and deliver in gold one thousand marks, with a warrant for a thousand loads of timber, to be taken out of her woods or elsewhere'. Within a month, Stow says, there was a temporary roof covering and 'the same year also the great roofs of the west and east ends were framed out of great timber in Yorkshire, brought thence to London by sea, and set up and covered with lead'. But so far as the steeple was concerned 'divers models were devised and made, but little else was done, through whose default God knoweth; it was said that the money appointed for new building of the steeple was collected'. A design exists for an elegant stone spire, by one John Shute of about 1580; and this must be one of the 'divers models' prepared.

Returning to the thirteenth century, we must trace the story of the building of the Gothic choir. On the feast of St Remigius in 1241 there was a great dedication of the cathedral, as it then existed; but this dedication cannot have been of the choir as shown in Hollar's engravings and in the drawings which Wren had made before the Great Fire of 1666. It was surely a dedication of the choir in its former late Romanesque manifestation, together with the completely vaulted nave and transepts, and the early thirteenth-century realization of the west front. Also quite recently completed were the stalls in the choir, the bishop's throne, and the bell tower.

Stow says that the 'new work' of St Paul's began in 1256; and it seems not to have been completed until the early fourteenth century, since Bishop Baldock (d. 1313) left a good deal of money for 'the finishing thereof'. What we see in Hollar's engravings and plan is as follows: first of all a magnificent thirteenth-century crypt, with immense clustered piers and groin vaults. A screen divided the crypt into two equal portions. At the east end was a chapel dedicated to the Holy Name of Jesus (a devotion maintained in the eastern chapel of the crypt at Canterbury). The western part was allowed for the use of parishioners of St Faith's parish church, which had to be demolished to make way for the new choir, and this chapel was called 'St Faith under St Paul's'. The eastern part of Wren's new cathedral continued to be used by

Hollar's engraving of the twelve-bay choir looking east, showing the arrangement of seating and other furnishings as it existed in the mid-seventeenth century.

13

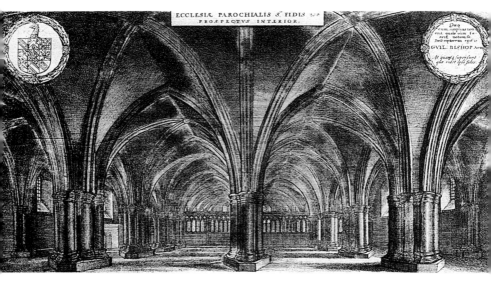

Hollar's engraving of the thirteenth-century eastern crypt.

St Faith's parish, and is still known by this name (though it is also, today, the Chapel of the Most Excellent Order of the British Empire).

The thirteenth-century choir was twelve bays long. Under the four western bays of the choir, west of the thirteenth-century crypt, the Romanesque crypt remained. These first four bays of the choir east from the crossing are thought to mark the eastward extent of the Romanesque choir, before the ambulatory and apse began. At this point, the fifth bay was wider than the four bays to the west or the seven bays to the east. Why this was so is not clear. It cannot have been to make a transition between one phase of work and another, for all the other bays are to all intents and purposes identical (irrespective of the order in which they were built). Was it for a liturgical reason? These bays seem to have contained double doors leading into the choir aisles, and so presumably provided the processional routes to and from the shrine of St Erkenwald which—on completion of the Gothic phase—was to be relocated, in another new shrine, behind the stone screen which closed off the high sanctuary and altar. Hollar's engraving shows the shrine in the form in which it survived until the Great Fire.

As completed, the choir provided accommodation for the

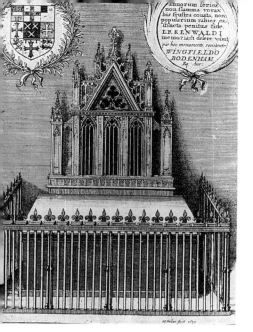
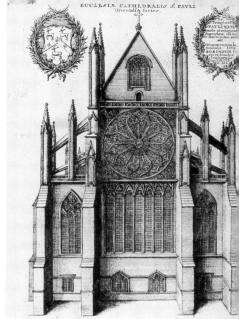

Two of Hollar's engravings from Sir William Dugdale's History of St Paul's
Cathedral *(1658)*.
LEFT: The altar and shrine of St Erkenwald.
RIGHT: The east front of the cathedral, showing the seven-light east window with a
rose window above.

singing choir and sanctuary, that is for the main musical and
liturgical focus of the daily sung Mass. This accounted for
seven bays, counting from the crossing. The altar and its screen
projected a certain distance into the eighth bay; two more bays
provided the setting for St Erkenwald's shrine and the pilgri-
mages and devotions relating to it. This left two final bays,
which were screened off right across the church to form the
Lady Chapel.

Over the Lady Chapel altar rose a fitting climax to the
whole building, namely a huge seven-light window with
cusping at the top of each light; and then, above a surprisingly
narrow division or transom, an enormous rose window, which
recalled that of Notre Dame in Paris. Fashionable shoemakers
of London imitated the tracery-work in cut-out work on their
footwear, and Chaucer's parish clerk had 'Paules windows
carven on his shoes'.

This, then, was the building which (though without its spire
from 1561) would have dominated all views of London from
the early fourteenth century until the third quarter of the
seventeenth. But St Paul's was still more than this, for it was

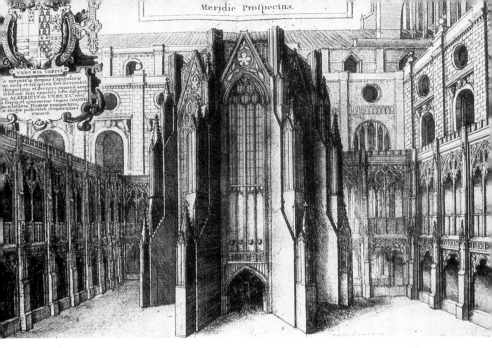

Hollar's engraving of the Chapter House and cloister by William de Ramsey, begun in 1332.

surrounded by subsidiary structures, quite apart from those which flanked the churchyard and formed the precinct of the cathedral. First in importance was the Chapter House and the two-storey cloister which enclosed it, west of the south transept (and entered from it) and on the south side of the nave. The deeds by which the bishop, Dean and Chapter set aside the site for this purpose and the indulgences which they offered to all who assisted in the work are dated 14, 15 and 17 June 1332; they state that the building work (designs for which must therefore have been prepared already) must begin at once and be pressed on to completion.

Hollar's view is the only illustration of this important structure we have. It shows with some thoroughness the design of the traceried openings of the two-storey cloister bays and the composition of the decorative elements on the surface. It shows, too, the decoration and window tracery of the Chapter House itself with its colossally tall upper chamber, and the tall, four-light windows above elongated blank traceried panels. Above the windows are steep gables, enclosing a cinquefoil within a circle and elongated trilobes. The tall, cut-off buttresses at the top would have formerly supported crocketed pinnacles, like those lower down. The architectural signifi-

cance of the Chapter House and cloisters is that, taken together, all the key elements of Perpendicular architecture are present. These can be seen not only in Hollar's engraving, but also in some of the numerous architectural fragments which remain and which are stored in the south gallery (over the south aisle) of the present cathedral.

The architect who designed the Chapter House and cloisters was William de Ramsey, who was working at St Stephen's chapel, Westminster, in 1323 and who died, probably of the Black Death, in 1349. He was undoubtedly one of the foremost architectural designers of his time, and from 1 June 1336 he was named by royal patent chief mason of the King's works in the Tower and other castles south of the River Trent. He nevertheless continued with his private practice, as a leading master mason and designer and, in particular, with the work he had contracted to do for the Bishop of London and the Dean and Chapter of St Paul's, in 1332. He had a close association with that part of the City in which he lived, the Ward of Aldersgate, and in 1347 he was its Common Councillor (that is, he sat on the governing body of the City of London, presided over by its Lord Mayor).

On the north side of the cathedral, at the west, was the Bishop of London's palace. East of this was the Pardon Churchyard, surrounded by its own cloister, on whose walls was a famous series of paintings of the 'Dance of Death'. Still further east was the College of the Minor Canons, where some of the junior clergy lived. Then came Paul's Cross. Paul's Cross was one of the great institutions of the City of London, for round this open-air pulpit men and women of all stations in life gathered to hear important proclamations made, to listen to sermons, and sometimes to witness show trials or other political events. Its origins seem to have been connected with the use of this part of the cathedral churchyard for the folkmoots or general gatherings of the people of the City; and it is first mentioned in 1191. Paul's Cross was several times rebuilt or repaired, most magnificently by Bishop Thomas Kempe in 1448. This was still standing at the time Stow was writing, in the late sixteenth century. A painting belonging to the Society of Antiquaries shows how it appeared in c. 1616, with a congregation assembled to hear a sermon. A two-tiered gallery is shown against the north side of the choir, with the Lord Mayor and other civic dignitaries sitting in the lower tier and King James I and his family in a kind of royal box above. The

painting was made by John Gipkyn to the commission of
Henry Farley, who had become greatly concerned by the
dilapidated condition of the cathedral at about that time, and
had printed appeals for money to repair the fabric. He
successfully persuaded James I to take an interest in the matter,
which led to the King coming in state to St Paul's to discuss
with the Lord Mayor, bishop and cathedral clergy what might
be done about it. Paul's Cross was pulled down on the orders
of the Long Parliament in 1643, and its original site is still
marked. The present Paul's Cross on a new site nearby is more
in the nature of a commemoration of the original than a
recreation of it.

By the last years of the sixteenth century the condition of the
Gothic cathedral was giving cause for real concern but, apart
from repairing the damage caused by the fall of the spire,
nothing substantial appears to have been done in Elizabeth's
reign. However, in July 1608, James I approached the Lord
Mayor and the Bishop of London, urging them to have the
cathedral properly surveyed and to prepare proposals for the
restoration of the fabric and the construction of a new spire to
be, at last, the successor to the one destroyed in 1561. It is not
clear whether the survey was made or, if so, by whom; but
two drawings survive from that time by the court architect
Inigo Jones (1573–1652). One drawing at Worcester College,
Oxford, shows a proposal for adding to the thirteenth-century
central tower a top storey in the form of an arcaded loggia. At
the four corners are shown octagonal turrets surmounted by
spirelets. Between the tops of the turrets and the spirelets are
volutes, and a ring of obelisks. The central feature is a very
curious ogival dome surmounted by a balustraded gallery,
again with obelisks; and higher still is a further gallery, more
obelisks, and finally a central spirelet topped off by a ball and
cross. It all looks very impractical. The other drawing, in the
Drawings Collection of the Royal Institute of British Architects, is a design for a new west front. It bears some relation to
what was actually carried out a quarter of a century later,
insofar as there are towers with octagonal turrets and spirelets
at the north-west and south-west corners, and prominent
volutes linking the central salient to the turrets. However,
nothing happened at this stage. In 1620 Charles I appointed a
Royal Commission to consider what might be done. Nothing
was, until the energetic William Laud became Bishop of
London in 1628. A new commission was galvanized into

Inigo Jones's drawing of c. 1610 showing his proposed capping of the thirteenth-century lantern tower, not carried out.

action, and in 1633 work started under the direction of Inigo Jones.

According to the eighteenth-century antiquary, George Virtue, Wren had information that Inigo Jones had started his career as an apprentice joiner in St Paul's Churchyard. However, the earliest record of him is as a 'picture maker' or painter, and he somehow acquired the opportunity of spending a considerable period, early in his life, in Italy. Between 1605 and 1640, back in England, his main work was in the designing and staging of masques, plays and other entertainments. A second Italian visit took place in 1613–14, as a member of the entourage of the Earl of Arundel, a generous patron and a passionate collector of art with a strong interest in Classical antiquities. Inigo Jones made use of this opportunity to acquire a detailed knowledge of the theory and grammar of Classical architecture. His annotated copy of Palladio's *Quattro*

Hollar's engraving showing the Gothic lantern tower rising above Inigo Jones's recasing of the nave, transepts and western towers. The west front is dominated by Inigo Jones's mighty portico, with figure sculptures of James I and Charles I. To its right is St Gregory's church, and behind St Gregory's the cloisters and the Chapter House.

Libri survives, and he brought back with him an extensive collection of engravings, books, and drawings, among them a large group of drawings by Palladio. In late 1615 he became Surveyor-General of the King's Works. In the reign of James I he designed the Banqueting House in Whitehall, the Queen's House at Greenwich, and the chapel by St James's Palace. All these, happily, still survive. By comparison, the work he did for old St Paul's is scarcely acknowledged. Even where it has been known and written about, it has been under-valued— except for the praise accorded to the noble portico. Yet between 1625 and 1640, and apart from his designing of the piazza and church of St Paul's, Covent Garden, for the Earl of Bedford, he was chiefly preoccupied with his large-scale works

at St Paul's Cathedral, and the result may fairly be claimed as being amongst his highest achievements.

Under Jones's direction the north and south walls of the nave, transepts and, above all, the west front were refaced with new masonry in Portland stone, so that the cathedral became a fascinating mixture of Classical and Gothic. It is shown from the south in one of Hollar's engravings. By contrast, the eastern arm was sensitively repaired with Gothic detailing, showing an empathy with the original architecture such as Wren himself was later to show in his large-scale work of repair and refacing of the stonework at Westminster Abbey.

The outstanding feature of Inigo Jones's work was the west portico, paid for by Charles I out of the privy purse, and it was the portico which both contemporaries and later historians have chiefly admired. But the portico was not something designed in isolation, rather it was an essential and powerful element in his conception for the whole west front. As the illustration shows, the new façade had north-west and south-west towers, outside the width of the aisles. These were topped by prominent cornices and then capped by set-back octagonal turrets with tapering spirelets. The Romanesque division into nave and aisles was still reflected in the façade by the classically inspired doorways. The pointed gable, with its stately pair of obelisks, did not look much like a Classical pediment, but the heroic Corinthian portico nevertheless tied the whole of the west façade together. The columns were approximately 45 feet (15 metres) high, and above them was a massive entablature, and then a balustraded parapet, making it the tallest portico north of the Alps. On the parapet ten large figure sculptures were projected, but only two were executed before the Civil War; they were of James I and Charles I and not, therefore, destined to last for very long. Apart from the details already mentioned, the whole façade was powerfully rusticated. It must have made a very strong impression as one approached up Ludgate Hill.

Such was the nature and appearance of the cathedral at the outbreak of the Civil War: Romanesque, early and late Gothic, and Inigo Jones's Classical language all co-existed side by side. This was the building which Sir Christopher Wren was to study, both to admire and to criticize: and which he would, eventually, replace.

Chapter Two

SIR CHRISTOPHER
WREN
(1632–1723)

A SUMMARY OF HIS LIFE
AND ACHIEVEMENTS

W REN WAS BORN on 20 October 1632 in the rectory at
East Knoyle, Wiltshire. His father, the Revd Dr Christopher
Wren, was a leading High Church clergyman who subsequently became Dean of Windsor, and his mother was Mary
Cox, who came from Fonthill, also in Wiltshire. His father's
brother, Matthew, was successively Bishop of Hereford, Norwich and Ely; and it was for his uncle, as Bishop of Ely and
Visitor of the College, that Wren in 1663–5 designed his first
work in architecture, the chapel of Pembroke College, Cambridge.

His early education was with a private tutor but, for a while,
Wren attended Westminster School in the time of one of its
most famous headmasters, Dr Busby. Then followed three
further years of private study before he went up to Wadham
College, Oxford, in 1649. Another important early influence
on Wren was his brother-in-law, the Revd Dr William
Holder, who 'initiated him in the Principles of Mathematicks',
and who later became a canon of St Paul's. Together with his
wife Susanna, Wren's sister, he lies buried in the crypt of the
present cathedral.

By this time Wren's family was caught up in the toils of the

Civil War, and the family took refuge with the Holders at their rectory at Bletchingdon, near Oxford. This was a less conspicuous place for a royalist family than the Deanery at Windsor.

At Oxford Wren came into contact with an outstanding group of scientific and mathematical scholars, who later formed the nucleus of what was to become the Royal Society in the reign of Charles II. They included Dr Charles Scarborough (a celebrated physician and mathematician), Dr John Wilkins (Warden of Wadham College, and afterwards Bishop of Chester), Dr Seth Ward (Savilian Professor of Astronomy, and afterwards Bishop of Salisbury), Robert Boyle (the physicist) and John Wallis (a distinguished mathematician).

Wren's astonishing precocity and range of intellectual interests were such that, at the age of sixteen, he had already taken part in significant anatomical experiments, drawn up an original astronomical thesis, and translated into Latin the section on *Geometrical Dialling* (sundials remained an interest of his) in William Oughtred's treatise *Clavis Mathematica*. *Parentalia* records his interest in model-making and in the devising of ingenious experiments to test his own or his friends' theories. At the age of nineteen he composed an algebraic tract 'of great use in Chronology'. In 1650 he took his BA degree, in 1653 his MA, and in the latter year was elected a Fellow of All Souls' College. He continued his wide-ranging scientific studies to such acclaim that, in 1657, he was chosen (apparently with Oliver Cromwell's support) to be Professor of Astronomy at Gresham College, London; and then, in 1660, he became Savilian Professor of Astronomy at Oxford. In the same year, the Restoration of the monarchy (to whose cause the Wren family had remained loyal) removed a major shadow from their lives, and Bishop Matthew Wren was one of those who were released from prison in the Tower of London. In Charles II the country had gained a ruler who was genuinely gifted, and who had a real and lively interest in the arts including architecture as well as in all manner of scientific and philosophical speculation and experiment. As *Parentalia* put it, 'the Royal Society had its beginning in that wonderful pacifick Year 1660, and as it began in that Time, when the kingdom was freed from Confusion and Slavery; so, in its Progress, its chief Aim has been to redeem the Minds of Men from Obscurity, Uncertainty, and Bondage'.

Soon after the Restoration the first real hints of Wren's

PARENTALIA:

OR,

MEMOIRS

OF THE

FAMILY of the WRENS;

VIZ. OF

MATHEW Bishop of ELY,

CHRISTOPHER Dean of WINDSOR, &c.

BUT CHIEFLY OF

SIR CHRISTOPHER WREN,

Late SURVEYOR-GENERAL of the Royal Buildings,
President of the ROYAL SOCIETY, &c. &c.

In which is contained, besides his WORKS,

A great Number of ORIGINAL PAPERS and RECORDS;

ON

RELIGION, POLITICKS, ANATOMY, MATHEMATICKS, ARCHITEC-
TURE, ANTIQUITIES; and most Branches of Polite Literature.

Compiled, by his Son CHRISTOPHER;
Now published by his Grandson, STEPHEN WREN, Esq;
With the Care of JOSEPH AMES, F.R.S. and Secretary to the Society of Antiquaries, LONDON.

LONDON:
Printed for T. OSBORN, in Gray's-Inn; and R. DODSLEY, in Pall-Mall.
MDCCL.

The title page of Parentalia, *compiled by Christopher Wren (son of the architect) from original documents and published by his son Stephen in 1750.*

developing interest in architecture occurred. A list in *Parentalia* of 'Theories, Inventions, Experiments and Mechanick Improvements' presented by Wren in his rooms at Wadham College included 'New Designs tending to Strength, Convenience and Beauty in Building', and considerable evidence of a serious scientific interest in the military arts of fortification, which relate closely both to architecture and to engineering.

Perhaps it was these theories that caused Charles II, in 1661, to invite Wren to supervise the fortification of Tangier (which had come to him as part of Catherine of Braganza's dowry), and at the same time to accept the reversion of Sir John Denham's post as Surveyor-General of the King's Works. Wren refused the opportunity to go to Tangier on grounds of ill-health, but it is clear that he continued to be held in high regard by the King. In 1663 the Archbishop of Canterbury, Gilbert Sheldon, recommended Wren to the King in a fresh context, to be one of three independent architects to advise a new Royal Commission examining the parlous condition of the fabric of old St Paul's. Meanwhile, Archbishop Sheldon himself had already commissioned Wren to design his second architectural enterprise—the Sheldonian Theatre in Oxford, given by Sheldon to provide a worthy setting for degree ceremonies and other formal university occasions. It was built 1664–9 after the pattern of learned antique precedents which were, of course, open to the sky; the Sheldonian Theatre had perforce to have a roof covering, and so Wren devised a special timber truss to cover the wide space without having recourse to columns.

In the year of the Great Plague, 1665, Wren made his only known visit abroad. As a letter quoted in *Parentalia* makes clear, his chief object in making the expedition was to busy himself 'in surveying the most esteem'd Fabricks of Paris, and the Country round; the Louvre for a while was my daily Object, where no less than a thousand Hands are constantly employ'd in the Works; some in laying mighty Foundations, some in raising the Stories, Columns, Entablements, &c. with vast Stones, by great and useful Engines; others in Carving, Inlaying of Marbles, Plaistering, Painting, Gilding, &c. which altogether make a School of Architecture, the best probably, at this Day in Europe.' In other words he was deliberately and comprehensively preparing himself for whatever lay ahead for him in this field; though he cannot have foreseen that the Great Fire, in the following year, would give him unprecedented opportunities for putting this experience to good use.

Following the Fire, Wren was immediately and irretrievably caught up in the architectural limelight of his time. Together with Roger Pratt and Hugh May he was appointed by the king one of three Commissioners, with three other nominees from the City, to survey the extent of the damage and to advise on how best the City should be rebuilt. It is a pardonable inaccuracy on the part of *Parentalia* to say that he was 'appointed Surveyor-general and principal Architect for rebuilding the whole City'. However, quite apart from his involvement with St Paul's, he was certainly an influential presence there, and assisted by Robert Hooke (Professor of Geometry at Gresham College) and Edward Woodroffe (who became his assistant surveyor at St Paul's) he was responsible overall for the rebuilding of fifty-two churches in the City. The cost of the fabric of the City churches was met by a tax on coals coming into the port of London, as the building of St Paul's was also to be financed after 1675. The furnishings and fittings, many examples of which remain, were probably in most cases designed by the master craftsmen who made them: Wren had a special rapport with the craftsmen in wood, stone and plaster, whom he regarded as his true colleagues and collaborators. The towers, mostly built towards the end of the century or even later, include some of the most felicitous inventions of the English Baroque period; collectively they still form a remarkable series and a punctuation of the City skyline (though no longer from so far away). The depredations of nineteenth-century bishops of London (who demolished a number, in spite of protests, so that they could use the proceeds of their sites to build new churches in the newly populous suburbs) and the destruction of others in the Second World War mean that there are now far fewer. Several churches are indeed substantial reconstructions following war damage. One has even been re-erected in Fulton, Missouri, in the United States of America. But, within walking distance of St Paul's, the following are especially rewarding: St Benet, Paul's Wharf (1677–83); St Edmund, King and Martyr, Lombard Street (1670–9; spire after 1708); St James, Garlick Hill (1676–83; spire 1713–17); St Martin Ludgate (1677–84); St Mary Abchurch (1681–6); St Mary-at-Hill, Thames Street (1670–6); and, above all, St Stephen, Walbrook (1672–9). St Vedast, Foster Lane (1670–3; tower 1694–7) and St Mary-le-Bow, Cheapside (1671–3; steeple 1680) are both near St Paul's and worth visiting too, but in both cases as much for their post-War restoration as for Wren's original work.

In the post-Fire City of London Wren also built a new Custom House (1669–71), itself destroyed by a fire in 1814; and the celebrated Monument to the Great Fire, in Fish Street Hill, seems to have been a collaboration between Wren and Hooke.

Wren may virtually be said to have pioneered the specialist profession of the 'conservation architect', with his surveys of Salisbury and Ely cathedrals, and of the Royal Peculiars of St George's Chapel, Windsor, and Westminster Abbey. *Parentalia* prints his reports on Westminster Abbey and Salisbury; like his analysis of the problems of Old St Paul's, these are masterpieces of acute observation and concise expression. He also designed furniture for Salisbury Cathedral, and at Westminster Abbey extensive repairs were carried out under his Surveyorship between 1698 and 1722. In London one other important church, St James, Piccadilly (1676–84), was designed by him; and a small but perfectly preserved country church, Ingestre in Staffordshire, can be attributed to him on circumstantial as well as on stylistic grounds. (Most of Wren's buildings are extremely well documented.) As one of the Commissioners for the Building of Fifty New Churches, established by Act of Parliament in 1711, Wren put down his thoughts on paper as to the planning and arrangement of these churches, the majority of the twelve which were actually built being wholly or partly the responsibility of his disciple and one-time assistant, Nicholas Hawksmoor. In his famous 'Letter to a Friend' (who was also one of the Commissioners) Wren urged that there should be no burials in the churches themselves; that their location be 'as forward as possible into the larger and more open streets'; he advocated the use of Portland stone (as at St Paul's, and for most of the City churches) and oak or deal for timber structures, and lead for roof coverings; and that the churches should be of such a manageable size that 'all who are present can both hear and see. The Romanists, indeed, may build larger churches; it is enough if they hear the Murmer of the Mass, and see the Elevation of the Host, but ours are to be fitted for auditories.' Of special interest for study of St Paul's, too, is his emphasis on the correct use of lime for pointing and rendering: 'Chalk-lime is the constant Practice, which, well mixed with good Sand, is not amiss, though much worse than hard Stone-lime. The Vaulting of St Paul's is a Rendering as hard as Stone; it is composed of Cockle-shell-lime well beaten with Sand; the more Labour in the beating, the better and stronger the Mortar.'

In March 1669 Wren had become Surveyor-General of the King's Works, in succession to Sir John Denham. Of the two obvious rivals for this pre-eminent post Hugh May became Comptroller of the Works at Windsor Castle, and John Webb was already in charge at Greenwich; both these responsibilities were, in due course, to fall to Wren as well. But already his new responsibilities were incompatible with a parallel university career and so, in 1673, he resigned his professorship at Oxford. He was knighted on 14 November the same year, another instance of the King's signal favour. For Charles II he undertook repairs, alterations or additions at St James's Palace and Whitehall Palace, and began the building of a completely new palace in Winchester (1683–5), left unfinished at the King's death. For William III and Mary II he built new south and east ranges of superlative quality at Hampton Court Palace (1689–94) and reconstructed Kensington Palace (1689–96).

At Oxford and Cambridge Wren carried out other

important commissions besides those already mentioned. In particular, at Cambridge he built the chapel of Emmanuel College (1668–73) and the peerless library of Trinity College (1676–84), one of the finest library rooms of that or any other age; and at Oxford he was responsible for the design of the Garden Quadrangle of Trinity College (1668, 1682, and 1728) and Tom Tower, at the entrance to Christ Church (1681–2), a happy example of the adaptation of the Gothic style to suit particular circumstances.

Other Wren buildings in London included the Royal Observatory at Greenwich (1675–6), the Royal Hospital at Chelsea (1682–92), and the Great Hall, twin domes and colonnades at the Royal Hospital for Seamen, Greenwich (1696 onwards), and Marlborough House, St James's (1709–11) for the first Duke of Marlborough. Outside London there is only one substantial surviving country house which is probably by him, Winslow Hall in Buckinghamshire (1699–1702); and at Lincoln Cathedral there is the library he built for Dean Honeywood (1674–5), less spectacular than the library at Trinity, Cambridge, but still immensely appealing.

It must also be told, sadly, that in the latter part of his career Wren was the victim of some political manoeuvring, and lost his post of Surveyor-General of the King's Works in 1718 to William Benson, a minor figure in architecture to say the least. At the same time, his relationships with the clergy at St Paul's were less smooth than they had been for the first twenty years of building the cathedral. Set against this are the close and happy relationships he seems to have enjoyed with Charles II, Mary II (but not with her longer-lived husband), and Queen Anne. In retirement he lived on the Green at Hampton Court, in the official residence of the Surveyor; though he retained a small house in central London, too, from which he could revisit St Paul's. He died on 25 February 1723, in his 91st year, having (as he himself put it) 'worn out (by God's Mercy) a long life in the Royal Service, and having made some Figure in the World'. He was buried in the crypt of St Paul's, fittingly, with an epitaph of sublime appropriateness placed above his resting place.

Wren was a man whose qualities may be seen as quintessentially English, and even as quintessentially Anglican. He was sturdily independent in his thoughts and in his actions, as many of the writings reproduced in *Parentalia* show. He began his professional life in one field, astronomy, and he triumphed in

Wren's epitaph, over his burial place in the crypt of St Paul's. The last five words of the Latin text say (in translation): 'Reader, if you seek a memorial—look around you!'

another, architecture; though it must never be forgotten that his earlier achievements in the scientific field were far from negligible, and were the necessary background to his architectural genius. Wherever architecture is known and celebrated as both an art and a science (for it is both, and yet more than the sum of both) the name of Wren is revered, and ever will be revered. St Paul's is his undoubted masterpiece, the astonishing achievement of one man in one lifetime. To that story we must now turn.

WREN AND ST PAUL'S

During the Civil War, and the Commonwealth which followed, old St Paul's was not merely neglected but deliberately and cruelly vandalized. For a time it was used to stable soldiers' horses and once, in an astonishing act of sacrilege, the font was used for the mock baptism of a newborn foal. The money and materials amassed for further major repairs were confiscated and dispersed, the woodwork was burned for firewood, and 'the beautiful Pillars of Inigo Jones's Portico were shamefully hew'd and defaced for support of the Timber-work of Shops,

29

for Seamstresses, and other Trades; for which sordid Uses, that stately Colonade was wholly taken up, and defil'd. Upon taking away the inner Scaffolds, which supported the arched Vaults, in order to their late intended Repair, the whole Roof of the South-cross [transept] tumbled down; and the rest in several Places of the Church, did often fall; so that the Structure continued a woful Spectacle of Ruin, till the happy Restoration' (*Parentalia*, p. 273).

Following the Restoration in 1660 the first step taken at St Paul's, in 1662, was to fit out a temporary new choir at the east end of the building with a wall dividing it from the rest, so that the daily worship of the cathedral could take place in safety. Then, in April 1663, a new Royal Commission was appointed. The Commissioners were given powers to recover the alienated property of the cathedral, to raise funds, and to call to their aid surveyors and craftsmen to help them 'search, discover, try, and find out the true state of the said church and the particular decays thereof'. Having established what needed to be done, they were empowered to put the work in hand and to supervise its execution.

The Commissioners were advised by Sir John Denham, Surveyor-General of the Royal Works—who had in turn consulted John Webb, the surviving disciple and former assistant to Inigo Jones, and Edward Marshall, the Master Mason to the Crown—that the central tower would have to be taken down and rebuilt from the foundations up, a drastic and expensive step. At this point Wren entered the picture for the first time, for the Commissioners decided to consult three other architects. Wren was recommended to them by the new Archbishop of Canterbury, Dr Gilbert Sheldon, for whom Wren was building the Sheldonian Theatre in Oxford; and the other two were Hugh May, Paymaster of the Royal Works, and Roger Pratt, a cultivated and well-travelled gentleman architect engaged principally in building country houses.

Pratt recommended a thorough patching up of the building as it was, including the central tower. With Hugh May in charge, some preliminary works were put in hand including the repair of Inigo Jones's portico, the demolition of encroaching houses, the amassing of building materials, and further assessments of the problems.

During this time, Wren was engaged upon a profound study of the medieval fabric and its structural defects. He began by making 'an exact Plan, Orthography, and Section, upon an accurate Survey of the whole Structure, even to Inches; in the Prosecution of which, he was astonish'd to find how negligent the first Builders had been' (*Parentalia*, p. 273). In the summer of 1665 all work on the cathedral ceased, while London suffered the worst attack of bubonic plague in its history. Wren, meanwhile, was on his study tour of Paris and its environs, and a new Dean of St Paul's, Dr William Sancroft, had taken office.

On Wren's return in the spring of 1666 he drew together the ideas which had been gestating in his mind since he was first approached in 1663, and wrote a succinct report (reproduced in *Parentalia*). He pointed out that whereas some advisers might recommend an extravagant approach to the repair of the cathedral 'which neither the Disposition, nor Extent of this Age will probably bring to a Period', others (and perhaps he was especially mindful of Roger Pratt) 'may fall so low as to think piecing up the old Fabrick, here with Stone, there with Brick, and cover all Faults with a Coat of Plaister, leaving it still to Posterity, as a further Object of Charity'. With consummate diplomacy and reasonableness he went on: 'I suppose your Lordships may think proper to take a middle Way, and to neglect nothing that may conduce to a decent uniform Beauty, or durable Firmness in the Fabrick, or Suitableness to the Expence already laid out on the Outside: especially since it is a Pile both for Ornament and Use'. He proceeded to enumerate not only the problems of repair but also the 'Defects of Comeliness' so that 'the one may be reconcil'd with the other in the Restitution. And yet I should not propose any Thing of meer Beauty to be added, but where there is a necessity of rebuilding, and where it will be near the same Thing to perform well as ill' (*Parentalia* pp. 274 and 275).

With regard to the Romanesque nave, his observations suggested to him that the original builders had provided insufficient abutment for supporting the weight of the roof; and that the massive piers were already in some cases as much as six inches (15.25 cm) out of true. Moreover the piers were built of rather small stones and consisted of an outer skin within which is 'nothing but a core of small Rubbish-stone, and much Mortar, which easily crushes and yields to the Weight'.

Just as Inigo Jones had totally refaced the Romanesque exterior, so Wren proposed to do the same internally 'after a good Roman manner', and to provide new vaults of brick (for lightness) plastered with stucco.

Coming to the crucial problems of the central tower, Wren regarded it as 'defective both in Beauty and Firmness'. The settlement of one of the piers had caused it to lean, and new arches had been inserted to support it, obscuring the views through the crossing. 'It must be concluded', he wrote, 'that the Tower from Top to Bottom, and the next adjacent Parts, are such a Heap of Deformities, that no judicious Architect will think it corrigible, by any Expense that can be laid out upon new dressing it, but that it will remain unworthy the rest of the Work, infirm and tottering; and for these Reasons, as I conjecture, was formerly resolv'd [i.e. by Denham, Webb and Marshall] to be taken down'. The solution which he then proposed is breathtaking in its originality, and prophetic in its foreshadowing of what would be raised forty years later as the culminating feature of new St Paul's: 'I cannot propose a better Remedy, than by cutting off the inner Corners of the Cross, to reduce this middle Part into a spacious Dome or Rotundo, with a Cupola, or hemispherical Roof, and upon the Cupola, (for the outward Ornament) a Lantern with a spiring Top, to rise proportionably, tho' not to that unnecessary Height of the former Spire of Timber and Lead burnt by Lightning' [in 1561].

The passage in which Wren outlines the advantages of this course of action is one of the most eloquent in all his surviving writings. Apart from the aesthetic attraction of a dome and lantern 'with incomparably more Grace in the remoter Aspect, than it is possible for the lean Shaft of a Steeple to afford', the expense would be hardly greater than the tricky business of properly reinstating the tower and its spire; and just as, in Inigo Jones's time, his great west portico 'being an intire and excellent Piece, gave great Reputation to the Work in the first Repairs, and occasion'd fair Contributions; so to begin now with the Dome may probably prove the best Advice, being an absolute Piece of itself, and what will most likely be finished in our Time; will make by far the most splendid Appearance; may be of present Use for the Auditory, will make up all the outward Repairs perfect; and become an Ornament to his Majesty's most excellent Reign, to the Church of England, and to this great City, which it is a pity, in the Opinion of our

OPPOSITE: *Wren's pre-Fire design for old St Paul's (1666) showing a dome, in replacement of the central crossing tower, and Inigo Jones's treatment of the nave, aisles and transept extended eastwards to encase the Gothic choir.*

Neighbours, should longer continue the most unadorn'd of her Bigness in the World'.

The report was presented to the Commissioners on 1 May 1666. Wren knew that he already had the moderate support of Hugh May and the implacable opposition of Roger Pratt. Wren returned to Oxford, while the Commissioners deliberated upon his recommendations. Finally, a meeting of all the Commissioners and their several advisers was fixed for Monday 27 August that year. One of the Commissioners was John Evelyn, a connoisseur of architecture, a leading expert on forestry and garden design, and famous today (like Samuel Pepys) as a diarist of his times. He gives in his diary a gripping account of this meeting, which concludes: 'When we came to the steeple, it was deliberated whether it were not well enough to repair it only on its old foundations, with reservation to the four pillars; this Mr. Chicheley and Mr. Pratt were also for, but we totally rejected it, and persisted that it required a new foundation, not only in regard of the necessity, but for that the shape of what stood was very mean, and we had a mind to build it with a noble cupola, a form of church building not as yet known in England, but of wonderful grace. For this purpose we offered to bring in a plan and estimate, which, after much contest was at last assented to, and that we should nominate a committee of able workmen to examine the present foundation. This concluded, we drew up all in writing, and so went with my Lord Bishop to the Dean's.'

Less than a week later, in the early hours of Sunday 2 September 1666, the Great Fire of London put paid to these plans. The fire began in Pudding Lane near London Bridge, and spread rapidly to the north and west. Because of its detached position in its churchyard, and the immense thickness of its walls, the cathedral seemed comparatively safe; and piles of belongings and of merchandise were heaped up in the churchyard and in the nave. The booksellers and stationers of Paternoster Row deposited their stock in the crypt chapel of St Faith, whose doors were then sealed and windows covered up. But on Tuesday morning the roof of the cathedral caught fire. Molten lead from the roofs, and burning timbers and masonry from the vaults, fell with such force that the vaulting of the crypt was smashed and the booksellers' stock added fuel to the flames. The cathedral was, from that moment, effectively lost.

By now Wren was the indispensable architectural adviser to the Dean and Chapter. As soon as it was practicable he fitted up for them at the west end of the nave a temporary choir in which, once more, the services could be held. For the remainder of 1666, the whole of 1667 and part of 1668 efforts were devoted to digging up the melted lead, clearing rubbish, taking down the walls of the most unsafe parts, and repairing the Chapter House (known then as the Convocation House).

At this stage, there seemed to be two chief options: to rebuild the old cathedral, with modifications, including (presumably) Wren's proposed central dome; or to start again and build a completely new cathedral, a daunting prospect indeed—especially when one considers the scale of rebuilding needed for the City of London as a whole, the distractions of the international political situation at that time, and the shortage of funds.

In the week following the fire, Wren had presented to the King his plan for rebuilding the city with a new cathedral and Royal Exchange as the focal points; and he had subsequently been appointed one of the Commissioners for the rebuilding of the city. His plan for a new cathedral showed in embryo what was to crystallize as the 'First Design', in which a domed assembly space or vestibule would be attached to a long rectangular choir with galleries north and south over covered arcades opening, at ground level, on to the churchyard.

However, there seemed to be some lingering reluctance entirely to abandon the old cathedral—for understandable reasons of history and sentiment as well as, perhaps, of expense—until there was a collapse in the roofless nave. This incident was reported in a vivid letter to Wren (who was in Oxford) from Dean Sancroft, dated 25 April 1668: 'What you whisper'd in my Ear at your last coming hither, is now come to pass. Our Work at the West-end of St. Paul's is fallen about our Ears. Your quick Eye discern'd the Walls and Pillars gone off from their Perpendiculars, and I believe other Defects too, which are now expos'd to every common Observer. About a week since, we being at Work about the third Pillar from the West-end on the South-side, which we had new cased with Stone, where it was most defective, almost up to the Chapitre [capital], a great Weight falling from the high Wall, so disabled the Vaulting of the Side-aisle by it, that it threatn'd a sudden Ruin, so visibly, that the Workmen presently remov'd; and the next Night the whole Pillar fell, and carry'd Scaffolds and all to the very Ground.' It appeared evident, at last, that Inigo Jones had made two structural mistakes: his external

casing of the clerestory walls was resting on the core of the
groins of the vaulting beneath, and there were no stones
keying in the new work with the old. Therefore, writes the
Dean, 'What we are to do is the present Deliberation, in which
you are so absolutely and indispensably necessary to us, that we
can do nothing, resolve on nothing without you'.

Sancroft's April letter was followed by another, equally
important, on 2 July 1668, written after a meeting he had had
with the Archbishop of Canterbury and the Bishops of
London and Oxford. 'They unanimously resolv'd, that it is fit
immediately to attempt something; and that without you they
can do nothing. I am therefore commanded to give you an
Invitation hither, in his Grace's Name, and the rest of the
Commissioners with all Speed; that we may prepare something to be propos'd to his Majesty (the Design of such a Quire
at least, as may be a congruous Part of a greater and more
magnificent Work to follow) and then for the procuring
Contributions to defray this . . .'. Evidently, in the intervening
correspondence, Wren must have asked how much money the
Commissioners thought would be available, so that he could
frame appropriate proposals with that sum in mind. With a
fine turn of phrase, Sancroft explained instead that 'quite
otherwise, the Way their Lordships resolve upon, is to frame a
Design handsome and noble, and suitable to all the Ends of it,
and to the Reputation of the City, and the Nation, and to take
it for granted, that Money will be had to accomplish it . . .'
(*Parentalia*, p. 279).

The choice of Wren as architect was made privately, in the
first place, by the Dean of St Paul's and the Archbishop of
Canterbury, and approved by the King. Subsequently it was
confirmed by the Commission as a whole, and Wren was
formally appointed to be in charge of building operations at St
Paul's with the title of Surveyor, and it is as 'the Surveyor' that
he is constantly referred to in *Parentalia*. To this day, the
architect responsible to the Dean and Chapter for the care of
the building is called the 'Surveyor to the Fabric'; and the
office has been held by a succession of distinguished practi-
tioners. In March 1669 Wren received the additional, and
significant, appointment as Surveyor-General of the Royal
Works, which not only gave him ultimate responsibility for
the upkeep of all Crown property but also brought within his
sphere of influence the royal stone quarries on the Isle of
Portland, which were to supply the bulk of the stone for the

new cathedral. Inigo Jones had used Portland stone for his Banqueting House in Whitehall, and for his remodelling of old St Paul's, and there seemed no doubt that it was a good weathering stone in the London environment. In addition it had a beautiful surface texture and tonality, and carved well.

By this stage the King had issued a royal warrant authorizing the Commissioners to demolish the old choir and tower 'in such a manner as shall be judged sufficient to make room for a new choir of a fair and decent fabric near or upon the old foundations'. A meeting was held to enlist the support of the City, with the Lord Mayor in the chair; and the scheme for building a new cathedral was warmly approved. The demolition of old St Paul's is referred to more than once by Samuel Pepys in his famous *Diary*, and of course in *Parentalia* (pp. 283–6): 'The pulling down of the Walls, being about 80 Feet high, and 5 Feet thick, was a great and troublesome Work; and the Men stood above, and work'd them down with Pickaxes, whilst Labourers below moved away the Materials that fell, and dispersed them into Heaps: the want of Room made this Way slow, and dangerous, and some Men lost their Lives; the Heaps grew steep and large; and yet this was to be done before the Masons could begin to lay the Foundations.'

Meanwhile, what foundations were to be laid? What would be the plans finally adopted? Progress, of various kinds, was being made. Dean Sancroft and Wren settled upon the old cloister area, with the Convocation House in the middle, as an appropriate place for a site office; and the Convocation House was repaired and adapted for this use.

The First Design, already referred to, was fully worked out by the end of 1669 and represented a complete break with Gothic tradition. Indeed it is difficult to find any precedent for it at all. The interior of the choir would have been something like the interior of St James, Piccadilly, only twice the length and with the spaces under the north, west and south galleries blocked off; from the outside, these spaces would have appeared as arcaded walks, in which the more secular aspects of life in the City could have gone on without disturbing the atmosphere of worship inside. At the west, Wren proposed a mighty assembly place under a dome, and a flight of steps leading up from it to the choir. Entrance to the domed space would have been through porticoes on the north, west and south sides—an aspect of the design specifically criticized by Roger Pratt. The London joiners, William and Richard Cleere, were commissioned to make a model of the design and in early 1670 it was put on display in the Palace at Whitehall so that the reactions of those closest to the King could be assessed. The choir section of the model, discreetly repaired, is on exhibition in the crypt of St Paul's, close to the Great Model.

The First Design was motivated by Wren's desire to provide something specifically fitted for Anglican worship—an 'auditory'—and at the most economical cost. But it did not win universal applause. Its scale was not what was hoped for, as the cathedral of a growing and increasingly confident capital city, and it departed too radically from expectations of what a cathedral should look like—not so much in its classical vocabulary as in its strange form.

In April 1670 Parliament passed a further *Act for Rebuilding the City* which contained some financial provision for the cathedral: on every chaldron or tun of coal landed at the Port of London an additional 2s. of duty was to be levied, and from 1 May 1s. 1$\frac{1}{2}d$. of the extra duty would go towards the rebuilding of fifty-one of the city churches, and 4$\frac{1}{2}d$. towards the building of new St Paul's. It was not a lot of money, but it would be a steady source of revenue. The direction of the whole ecclesiastical rebuilding programme was put in the hands of three Lords Commissioners, namely the Archbishop of Canterbury, the Bishop of London, and the Lord Mayor.

At this moment Wren became very strenuously involved with the programme for rebuilding the city churches, and sixteen were put in hand before the end of the year. A new deanery was built for Dean Sancroft and his successors, and Wren no doubt approved the design of it; though the detailed work was carried out by John Oliver, one of the City's surveyors, and Edward Woodroffe, Wren's deputy at St Paul's. Woodroffe also designed the three houses for residentiary canons at what was then called Amen Corner, but which is now part of Amen Court off Ave Maria Lane off Ludgate Hill.

In June 1672 the model of the First Design was carried back from Whitehall to St Paul's and placed in the Convocation House by four stout porters. There, on 12 July 1673, Roger Pratt saw it and—true to form and possibly not realizing that it had already been long superseded—he criticized it trenchantly. By this time, however, Wren had formulated fresh proposals based in plan on the form of a Greek cross, and these new proposals had even passed through more than one stage. This stage, for a centrally planned domed cathedral with four equal

Engraving of the Great Model design (perhaps engraved directly from the model, rather than from drawings), though wrongly labelled 'First Design': from an engraving inserted in the Dean and Chapter's copy of Parentalia.

arms, exists in a set of drawings. As in the First Design, steps lead up to monumental frontispieces on the north, west and south sides. A new feature was the introduction of concave quadrants on the diagonals, linking the four façades on the cardinal points. This feature was carried forward to the design we know both from drawings and from the Great Model, which is in essence the Greek cross design plus an extension to the west with a domed vestibule and a deep portico. The Great Model was made, like its predecessor, by William and Richard Cleere and we know that preparations for making it were in hand between April and September 1673. It cost over £500. Not only is the joinery superb, but the capitals, cherubs' heads, flowers and festoons are all beautifully carved. The King's Sergeant Painter, Robert Streeter, was paid for gilding certain details. Originally there were tiny figures on the parapets, thought to have been Wren's first commission to Grinling Gibbons, an exceptionally talented young sculptor who had been discovered, by John Evelyn, working in a cottage close to his house in Deptford in 1671.

On 12 November 1673, the King issued letters patent making it clear that he now regarded it as inevitable that the surviving remains of the old cathedral should be totally demolished and cleared away, and that a new cathedral should be built. In the preamble he stated that '. . . we have caused several Designs to that Purpose to be prepared by Dr. Christopher Wren, Surveyor General of all our Works and Buildings, which we have seen, and one of which we do more especially approve, and have commanded a Model thereof to be made after so large and exact a Manner that it may remain as a perpetual unchangeable Rule and Direction for the Conduct of the whole Work . . .' (*Parentalia*, pp. 280–1.)

Thus it appeared at this stage that the design incorporated in the Great Model was to be built. The King had very specifically and wholeheartedly approved of it and, in *Parentalia's* words, 'Some Persons of Distinction, skilled in Antiquity and Architecture, express'd themselves much pleased with the Design'; moreover, Wren himself 'in private Conversation, always seem'd to set a higher Value on this Design, than any he had made before or since; as what was labour'd with more Study and Success; and, (had he not been over-rul'd by those, whom it was his Duty to obey,) what he would have put in Execution with more Chearfulness, and Satisfaction to himself than the latter'. (*Parentalia*, p. 282.)

The next stages are crucial to an understanding of what actually happened, though by no means easy to discern. The Great Model design was abandoned, presumably because—as in the case of the First Design—its conception was so far distant from that of a traditional Gothic cathedral, with a choir for the daily services of the cathedral community, and a long nave for big congregational services, processions, and so forth. Perhaps also the Great Model, with its distinct echoes of Renaissance and Baroque Rome, was too 'Popish' for some tastes; or perhaps the clergy simply failed to grasp how they would be able to use it, both liturgically and practically. At any rate 'nothing could be fully resolv'd upon; the Chapter, and some others of the Clergy thought the Model not enough of a Cathedral-fashion; to instance particularly, in that, the Quire was designed Circular, &c. in the mean Time, the Money granted by Parliament upon the Coal-duty began to come in; something was to be done in order to make a Beginning without more Delay. The Surveyor then turn'd his Thoughts to a Cathedral-form, (as they call'd it) but so rectified, as to reconcile, as near as possible, the Gothick to a better Manner of Architecture; with a Cupola [dome], and above that, instead of a Lantern, a lofty Spire, and large Porticoes.'

WREN AND ST PAUL'S

The final paragraph of Dean Sancroft's April 1668 letter contains an intriguing reference, which seems to refer to plans either for rebuilding or for a new building which may be those—or closely similar to those—incorporated in the so-called Warrant Design of 1675: 'You will think fit, I know, to bring with you those excellent Draughts and Designs you formerly favour'd us with; and in the mean time, till we enjoy you here, consider what to advise, that may be for the Satisfaction of his Majesty, and the whole Nation'. (*Parentalia*, pp. 278–9.)

It seems unlikely that the Dean was referring to the plans prepared for the situation as it existed before the Great Fire. The Warrant Design, however, looks in several respects like a stage between the pre-Fire plans and what was afterwards adopted. It is on a Latin, cross plan, with choir, nave and transepts; the west towers stand outside the nave, as they did in the old cathedral; there is a deep portico, with sculptured figures over a balustrade, echoing Inigo Jones's; the dome is surmounted by a curious steeple (pagoda-like, in six diminishing stages, in contrast to the elongated cone above a lantern in the pre-Fire design): and, in a most compelling link with the pre-Fire building, the Warrant Design takes as its basic vocabulary the language of Inigo Jones's recasing of the nave and transepts with round-headed windows, at both aisle and clerestory level, and flat pilaster-strips between the bays.

On 14 May 1675 the King issued a royal warrant for making a start on the new cathedral. Noting that the duty on coals 'doth at present amount to a considerable Sum, which, tho' not proportionable to the Greatness of the Work, is notwithstanding sufficient to begin the same; and with all the Materials, and other Assistances, which may probably be expected, will put a new Quire in great Forwardness', the King dealt with the question of the design once more: 'whereas among divers Designs which have been presented to Us, we have particularly pitched upon one, as well because we found it very artificial [skilful], proper, and useful; as because it was so ordered that it might be built and finish'd by Parts: We do therefore by these Presents signify our Royal Approbation of the said Design, hereunto annexed; and do will and require you forthwith to proceed according to the said Design, beginning with the East-end or Quire . . .' (*Parentalia*, p. 281). The designs are still stitched to the warrant, preserved in the library of All Souls' College, Oxford.

Parentalia hints at a degree of disillusionment on Wren's part at this point, recording that he 'resolved to make no more Models, or publicly expose his Drawings, which, (as he had found by Experience,) did but lose Time, and subjected his Business many Times, to incompetent Judges'. The final sentence of this section, however, confirms a major royal concession: 'And the King was pleas'd to allow him the Liberty in the Prosecution of his Work, to make some Variations, rather ornamental, than essential, as from Time to Time he should see proper; and to leave the Whole to his own Management' (*Parentalia*, p. 283).

What this meant in practice was that Wren at once began to make substantial adjustments to the design. Perhaps the King knew already that he fully intended to do so, and was in effect protecting him from further uncreative interference. The building continued to evolve throughout its execution so that, for example, the precise forms of the dome and of the western towers were not settled upon until the early years of the eighteenth century, by which time the cathedral had been in continuous construction for more than a quarter of a century. It must be recalled, however, that Wren had constantly to report to the Commissioners for the Rebuilding of the Cathedral Church of St Paul, appointed in November 1673, and to secure their approval for the proposals as they developed, including the placing of contracts, and a multiplicity of other matters connected with the progress of the work. The Building Committee, in effect the executive committee of the Commissioners, met monthly in the early years of the building programme, and was usually attended by between six and ten Commissioners. This was the group of people, most of whom he knew well, to whom Wren worked.

The foundation stone of the new cathedral was at last laid on 21 June 1675, in the south-east corner of the building. Joshua Marshall, Master Mason to the Crown, and Thomas Strong, from Oxfordshire, were the first two masons to sign contracts for different parts of the work. It is a happy fact that for the building of St Paul's the documentation is exceptionally complete; we know precisely which teams were engaged upon which work, at what moment and at what cost.

In the preparations for the laying of the foundation stone a singularly auspicious omen presented itself. Wren himself was on site, establishing the dimensions of the dome upon the ground; having fixed upon the centre he called for a stone to mark the place, and a workman was sent to bring him a flat stone from a nearby heap of rubble. Wren turned it over in his hands, and saw that it was a fragment of a gravestone from the old cathedral. Carved on it, in large capitals, was the single Latin word RESURGAM: 'I shall rise again'.

Right from the beginning, changes were made from what was set out in the Warrant Design. In particular the outer walls were made 2 feet (60 cm) thicker, the aisles narrower, and the shape of the piers dividing the choir from its aisles changed. Instead of the pilaster-strips dividing one bay of the external elevation from another, coupled pilasters were substituted. Most significantly, the outer walls rose not just to the height of the aisles but to the full height of the nave and choir. Behind the outer walls (not visible, of course, from the ground) are enclosed areas above the roofs of the aisles, right round the building; and within these areas are flying buttresses, to counteract the thrust of the choir and nave vaults. Between the buttresses are the clerestory windows, which are clearly seen and form part of the architecture inside the building, but which are quite invisible from any normal viewpoint outside the building.

In October 1675 Edward Woodroffe died; he was replaced in the following year by John Oliver, who remained as Wren's deputy at St Paul's until 1701. In 1678 Joshua Marshall died, and was succeeded at St Paul's (and also as Master Mason to the Crown) by Thomas Wise. Two more principal contractors, Edward Pierce (who carved the superb bust of Wren now in the Ashmolean Museum, Oxford), and Jasper Latham, were brought in to speed up the work. In 1681 Thomas Strong was replaced by his younger brother, Edward. In this way the team of contractors and master craftsmen was gradually consolidated, with Wren establishing excellent working relationships with them, and carrying out a regular visit of inspection on Saturdays; both he and John Oliver regularly scrutinized and signed the accounts.

In 1687 the duty on coals was extended and, with work on the city churches well advanced, more of the money could be made available for the building of St Paul's. Two new master masons, Samuel Fulkes and Christopher Kempster, were awarded contracts; and work on the west end began in 1688.

A further modification to the concept of the Warrant Design was made in respect of the number of bays in the nave, which were reduced from five to three. Instead of the fourth and fifth bays, one larger bay was substituted, of magnificent proportions and covered inside by a saucer dome larger and more enriched than those over the other three bays. On either side it is flanked by the western chapels, over which on the north side is the Trophy Room (where the Great Model was kept for many years) and on the south side, over what is now the Chapel of St Michael and St George, is the Library. By 1687–8, £34,000—an immense sum—was being spent annually, a considerable increase on the period when the coal tax yielded comparatively little for St Paul's. By the time the final accounts were drawn up, in 1710, a total of £738,845, 5s. 2½d. had been spent. But early in 1697 Parliament, subject to pressure from those who thought the building of the cathedral was proceeding rather too slowly, suspended half of Wren's annual salary until such time as the work should be completed. On 2 December in that same year the fully furnished choir was brought into use for the first time, for a service of thanksgiving for the Peace of Ryswick. A special anthem was composed for the occasion by Dr John Blow; and the Bishop of London, Dr Henry Compton, who like Wren had been associated with the building of the cathedral since the beginning, mounted the pulpit for the very first time and delivered a sermon on a text from Psalm 121: 'I was glad when they said unto me, Let us go into the house of the Lord'. For the first time, also, he would have occupied the bishop's throne, sitting beneath a canopy carved by Grinling Gibbons, and on a magnificent chair which still survives.

The next part of the building to be brought into use was the Morning Chapel (now St Dunstan's Chapel, on the north side of the western vestibule), on 1 February 1699. Curtains of purple cloth, fringed with purple and crimson silk, were hung over Jonathan Maine's sumptuously carved screen, and purple cloth cushions were placed on the desks of the cathedral dignitaries. No altar table was installed, as the chapel was to be used solely for the morning office, but thirteen handsomely bound copies of the Book of Common Prayer (1662) were provided.

Meanwhile the exterior of the cathedral was reaching towards completion. The carving of the Royal Arms, supported by two angels 8 feet (2.4 metres) high in the pediment

The sumptuous chair of 1697 made in Grinling Gibbons's workshop for the Bishop of London's throne.

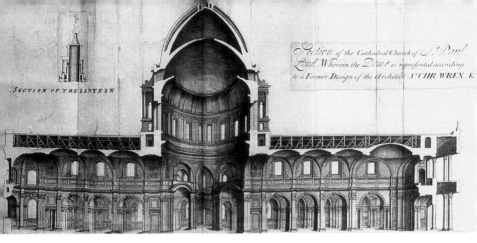

Engraving showing a section through St Paul's, largely as built except that the final form of the dome has still not been resolved. Presumably this was the penultimate stage. Engraving from the Dean and Chapter's copy of Parentalia.

of the north transept, was carried out by Grinling Gibbons; and the carving in the equivalent position on the south transept, of a phoenix rising from the flames with the word *Resurgam*, was done by Caius Gabriel Cibber. Cibber also carved the four large 'incense pots' or urns to stand on the gate piers at the bottom of the two flights of black marble steps which led down from the south portico doorway.

The drum of the dome was also rising, the final design of its culminating parts still in the future. It was not until 1704 that the design for the completion of the dome seems to have been finally settled. *Parentalia*, referring to what is there called the 'great Cupola', explained that since 'It was necessary to give a greater Height than the Cupola would gracefully allow within, though it is considerably above the Roof of the Church; yet the old Church having had before a very lofty Spire of Timber and Lead, the World expected, that the new Work should not in this Respect fall short of the old (tho' that was but a Spit, and this a Mountain). He was therefore oblig'd to comply with the Humour of the Age, (tho' not with ancient Example, as neither did Bramante) and to raise another Structure over the first Cupola; and this was a Cone of Brick, so built as to support a stone Lantern of an elegant Figure, and ending in Ornaments of Copper gilt. As the whole Church above the Vaults is covered with a substantial oaken Roof, and Lead, (for no other Covering is so durable in our Climate) so he covered and hid out of Sight the Brick Cone with another Cupola of Timber and Lead; and between this and the Cone are easy Stairs that ascend to the Lantern.' (*Parentalia*, p. 291.)

Two more valuable details are contributed at this point, by *Parentalia* (pp. 291 and 292). After referring to the paintings by Sir James Thornhill on the surface of the innermost dome, it states: 'In the Crown of the Vault, as in the Pantheon, is a circular Opening, by which not only the Lantern transmits its Light, but the Inside Ornaments of the painted and gilded Cone, display a new and agreeable Scene.' Furthermore, 'Altho' the Dome wants no Butment, yet, for greater Caution, it is hooped with Iron in this Manner; a Chanel is cut in the Bandage of Portland-stone, in which is laid a double Chain of Iron strongly linked together at every ten feet, and the whole Chanel filled up with Lead'.

The evolution of the precise design of the two western towers, and of the central west front of the cathedral, was also a prolonged process. For the west front the Warrant Design shows a projecting portico three bays deep and ten columns wide: above it is a pedimented attic with scrolly volutes at the sides, distinctly reminiscent of Inigo Jones's recasing of the old west front. The towers have a louvred belfry stage at clerestory level, capped by small attic stages and then pyramidal domes with finials in the shape of excessively tall slender urns with flames issuing forth. Wren explored the idea of a portico with a single giant order of columns, as in the Great Model design, and several drawings for such a scheme survive. *Parentalia* tells us that 'It is most certain his Intention and Desires from the Beginning' were to this end, but he was defeated by the inability of the Portland quarries to supply stones larger than a certain size, and hence he was unable to construct columns of sufficient dimensions. 'An Enquiry was made after all the good Stone that England afforded. Next to Portland, Rock-abbey Stone, and some others in Yorkshire seemed the best and most durable; but large Stone for the Paul's Works was not easily to be had even there.' Work on the west towers was carried on between about 1705 and 1708. The north-west tower was built by Samuel Fulkes, and the south-west (with its geometrical staircase) by Christopher Kempster (who also worked on the dome, as his handsome monument in Burford church in Oxfordshire proudly states). Unlike the rather tame Warrant Design versions, and those shown in engravings published between 1701 and 1703, the final stages of the towers are clearly influenced by the work of Francesco Borromini and are the most strongly Baroque elements in the entire building.

The last word must be *Parentalia*'s (pp. 292 and 293): 'The first Stone of this Basilica was laid in the Year 1675, and the Works carried on with such Care and Industry, that by the Year 1685 the Walls of the Quire and Side-ailes were finished, with the circular North and South Porticoes; and the great Pillars of the Dome brought to the same Height; and it pleased God in his Mercy to bless the Surveyor with Health and Length of Days, and to enable him to complete the whole Structure in the Year 1710 to the Glory of his most holy Name, and Promotion of his divine Worship, the principal Ornament of the Imperial Seat of this Realm . . . Thus was this mighty Fabrick, the second Church for Grandeur in Europe, in the space of 35 Years, begun and finished by one Architect, and under one Bishop of London, Dr Henry Compton: the Charge supported chiefly by a small and easy Imposition on Sea-coal brought to the Port of London . . .'.

Chapter Three

AN ARCHITECTURAL WALK ROUND THE EXTERIOR OF ST PAUL'S

A GOOD way to arrive at St Paul's, other than on foot up Ludgate Hill, is by Underground and then to walk along the north flank of the cathedral, with the cathedral on the left and the red-brick Chapter House on the right, so that you arrive at the west front with some sense of progression. A particularly spectacular view of the dome and the south transept can be had by crossing the road close to the circular building of the City Information Centre, and then by walking down Peter's Hill in a direct line away from the south transept. It is worth walking all the way down as far as you can go—and, incidentally, being rewarded with a view of the delightful Dutch-inspired red-brick church of St Benet, Paul's Wharf (also by Wren, 1677–83)—before retracing your steps.

The Baroque spectacle of St Paul's can be really well appreciated from the bottom of Peter's Hill. This is a view which is also especially beautiful at night, when the cathedral is flood-lit. It is also a good place to start from historically, for Paul's Wharf was where the boats unloaded the Portland stone used successively by Inigo Jones between 1625–40 and then by Sir Christopher Wren from 1675–1710. No doubt, also, the Caen stone from Normandy used for the construction of that part of the old cathedral begun in 1087 was also landed here or nearby. From Paul's Wharf a short street called Bennet Street

The west front of St Paul's from a high viewpoint showing the dome framed between the west towers, and the double-storey portico.

(Benet) led upwards to the final steep haul, which was called Paul's Chain and is now called Peter's Hill after a long vanished church called St Peter, Paul's Wharf.

The West Front

At length, the visitor arrives at the west front. However, by standing back as far as it is possible to do without actually walking down Ludgate Hill, you can take in the following. The façade of the cathedral is divided into two stages or storeys, both of immense height (53 feet or 16.2 metres for the lower storey, and 47 feet or 14.3 metres for the upper). The lower storey itself stands on a base, of heavily scored or rusticated masonry, which is the same height as the top of the steps (approximately 12 feet or 3.6 metres).

The centre of the façade is dominated by the mighty portico. As we have seen (p. 39) Wren had intended this to be a gigantic single-storey portico, perhaps in homage to the Inigo Jones portico of the 1630s, and it is shown in this form on the Great Model in the crypt; but stones of sufficient size were not available. Some writers have found the double-storey portico, by comparison, weak. It is a noble design, nevertheless, and one which is full of subtleties. The lower stage consists of six pairs of fluted Corinthian columns, supporting a colossal entablature which also forms the base for the upper storey. The frieze of the entablature is not of Portland stone but of white marble. The upper storey consists of four pairs of Composite columns: they are placed directly over the corresponding ones beneath but, because they are smaller in scale, they are slightly wider apart from one another. The entablature supported by these columns is enriched with fewer bands of ornament than the lower entablature (three, compared with five) but, as if to prepare for the splendours of the pediment above, it has a rhythmically regular tier of volutes (presenting a fluted or gadrooned surface to the front) and the overhang is coffered. Then comes the pediment, surmounted by a great figure of St Paul (carrying the sword which was the instrument of his execution) at the top, and figures of St Peter (with the cock, which crowed thrice) and St James, to left and right respectively. These three sculptures on the pediment, and the four equally fine sculptures of the four Evangelists on the west towers—Matthew, Mark, Luke and John—are all by that excellent sculptor Francis Bird (1667–1731), whose work we shall see elsewhere, both on the west front and in other parts of

Francis Bird's relief sculpture of the Conversion of St Paul.

the cathedral. As a very young man he went first to the Low Countries and then to Rome, where he studied under a sculptor called Le Gros; then, on returning to England, he worked with each of the two older sculptors whose work is also particularly well represented at St Paul's, Grinling Gibbons and Caius Gabriel Cibber. Framed by the pediment is a dramatic relief sculpture by Bird, for which he was paid £650 in December 1706, showing the *Conversion of St Paul*, illustrating the passage in the Acts of the Apostles which begins: 'And suddenly there shone round about him a light from heaven, and he fell to the earth, and heard a voice saying unto him "Saul, Saul, why persecutest thou me?" '

Within the upper stage of the portico is an airy gallery, which can be reached (though not in normal circumstances) ·from a small doorway in the large segmental-headed west window. One wonders whether Wren ever envisaged it being used as a place from which the Bishop of London might bless crowds of pilgrims gathered below, like the Pope from the balcony of St Peter's in Rome. It would make a no less dramatic setting.

The lower storey of the portico invites entrance to the cathedral, by leading the eye, and ultimately the visitor, in. This is achieved by subtle arrangement of spaces and further decorative enrichment, of which the principal constituents are the columns and their relationship with the giant pilasters attached to the wall behind, and the sculptured reliefs (all seven by Francis Bird).

The two inner pairs of columns create the drama and the sense of depth, for the central part of the west front is deeply recessed behind them. At the back of the recess in the centre is the west door, opened now only on special occasions. The door is flanked by a single pair of pilasters, and these are generously spaced so that one feels a sense of repose—of arrival, indeed—compared with the sense of expectation and excitement generated by the outer pairs of columns and pilasters. Above the door the central relief panel shows *Paul preaching to the people of Berea*. Left and right of the door, a little lower down and placed over deep niches, are smaller reliefs depicting, respectively, *Paul preaching on Mars' Hill in Athens* and *Paul before Agrippa*. The reliefs on the inner north and south walls of the portico, facing inwards, show *Paul converting the gaoler* and *Paul punishing Elymas the sorcerer*, while the reliefs over the subsidiary north and south doors show *The Stoning of Stephen* (in the Acts of the Apostles, at the point where the first martyrdom is described, we are told 'And the witnesses laid down their clothes at a young man's feet whose name was Saul', i.e. Paul before his conversion), and *Ananias restoring the sight of Saul*. Within the entrance portico, on the south wall, is a graffito which says 'JH 1701'.

Contemplating the towers once more, one notices that they naturally follow the division into storeys or zones established by the portico—and which ordinance now holds good for the rest of the cathedral. On the lower stage, reading from left to right, there is a projecting entablature above a pair of pilasters separated by a thin band of rustication. The eye is then taken inwards by a change of plane, and an inner order of pilasters frames a wide niche which in turn contains a window, much smaller than the niche. The head of the niche is panelled, in such a way as to create a deeper perspective, and the window is supported by an elegantly-judged composition, rather like the base of a church monument, in which two projecting panels— a smaller one on a larger one—produce an impression of dignified monumentality.

St Paul's is an intensely sculptural cathedral, and a particular pleasure lies in the way in which the ornament above the niche (and in countless similar situations) is managed: in the frieze a superb cherub's head enfolded in its own wings supports a

console or bracket, and left and right of it are motifs made up of a sword (for St Paul) and a Baroque trumpet (representing Fame) wreathed in laurel leaves. Below the frieze elaborate drops of flowers cascade along the spandrels to frame the head of the niche. In the entablature above, a tiny oval window is vividly brought to life by a frame of masks, draperies and curly volutes. Although such ornament is the stock-in-trade of Baroque architecture, as Wren knew well from his visit to France in 1665–6 and from his study of Dutch, German and Italian examples, they can rarely have been devised or executed with more virtuosity or panache.

The upper storey has a similar arrangement of pilasters, though the effect is lighter and calmer because there is no projecting portico towards the centre with columns in front of the pilasters. Instead of a niche as the central motif, however, there is an aedicule (like a miniature temple-front), a pediment supported on engaged columns. This encloses a taller rectangular window to light the bell-ringers' chamber behind; and there is space for a sculptured panel of floral swags below the window, and for bands of rustication on either side of the aedicule. Above the aedicule is a frieze with the shield of arms of the Dean and Chapter of St Paul's in the centre, with ribbons, and swags of foliage and flowers.

The two lower stages of the south tower correspond closely to the north, except for the lower frieze which has a cherub's head differently supported and looking towards the Old Deanery, flanked by sprays of tall palm leaves and swags of flowers. At the foot of the towers on the north and south sides are handsome doorways, that on the north leading to the Chapter House and that on the south, the Dean's Door, leading to the Old Deanery, which is just down the little street opposite. The carving over the Dean's Door incorporates a weeping cherub.

To complete the account of the west towers: above the entablature of the main west front rises, on either side, an attic stage of magnificent plain masonry with projecting panels or aprons at the corners. In the centre of all four faces is a circular opening, seemingly punched into the masonry with great force, and these 'portholes' are encircled with thin borders of acanthus leaves. On all four sides the cornice curves up over the circular openings, setting up a vigorous rhythm. On the north

OPPOSITE: A detail of the rich architectural sculpture of St Paul's: the winged cherub's head is a constantly recurring motif.

tower these openings have remained pierced, and serve as unusually magnificent bell-openings; on the south tower they are closed up, with clock faces on three of the four sides. At the foot of the attic stage at the front are the figures of the four Evangelists, already mentioned; and over the corners are urns, on stepped pyramids, with gilded acorns for their finials.

Above the attic stage the architecture becomes a whirling exercise in curves and concaves, diagonals and domes. The next, temple-like, stage is circular or would be but for the powerful interruption at all four corners of projecting porticoes placed diagonally over the diagonal points of the towers. The entablature is richly carved, and leads the eye up to the next stage, also circular, which has eight round-arched openings with keystones; however, the eye is tantalized by not being able to see all these, on account of the recessed attics over the projecting porticoes of the stage below. Both the porticoes and their attics have pairs of urns with carved flames (symbol of eternity) issuing from them, so the sense of excitement is redoubled.

The circular arcaded stage has a rippling entablature which would have done credit to Borromini. It is succeeded by a further attic stage with small segmental-headed windows, and powerful volutes between them.

Finally, it is the turn of the tall bell-like domes. Covered with lead, their drama is accentuated by the eight ribs and the oval rings (*trompe l'oeil* lucarnes or miniature window openings) on alternate panels. Above the domes burst the gilded finials: immense fronded pineapples, symbol of prosperity and peace, on tall, scrolly brackets. Then, the sky.

Returning to ground level, before circumnavigating the cathedral, the two flights of steps claim some attention. The lower flight was reconstructed by the then Surveyor to the Fabric, F C Penrose, in 1873, broadly following Wren's drawings; the upper flight is contained within low stone structures which, on their outer sides, contain entrances to the space under the stairs. Mounted on these projecting walls are wrought-iron standard lamps which, though convincingly in the style of Wren, were in fact designed by that great admirer of Wren, Sir Edwin Lutyens. The stone bases have weathered quite considerably in the relatively short time they have been there, which contributes to their looking older than they are. They were given by the Royal Academy, out of the fund established in Lord Leighton's memory, which has also paid for many of the monuments in the crypt to former Presidents of the Royal Academy.

In front of the cathedral is a sculpture of Queen Anne, in whose reign the cathedral was completed; she is shown standing and crowned, with a sceptre and orb in her hand, and subsidiary figures representing Great Britain, Ireland, France and America seated round the base. The whole group is surrounded by a railing. This pedestrian affair is by Richard Belt, and was provided in 1885 as a substitute for the decaying original by Francis Bird, which was rescued by the writer Augustus Hare and taken to his house, St Mary's Place, Holmhurst, near Hastings in Sussex, where it still remains. The cast-iron railings were newly provided in 1885 by Young and Co., iron-founders, of Pimlico. The original group was enclosed by a low curved wrought-iron rail by Tijou.

A careful study of the west front in this way provides one with a knowledge of the vocabulary for the whole building, and it is well worth the time spent.

The North Side of the Nave

From here it is recommended that the visitor take a clockwise route, as follows. From just below the steps leading to Paternoster Square (Paternoster Row was the street where, in the Middle Ages, the Paternosterers or rosary-makers had their workshops) one sees two important aspects of St Paul's, namely the western bay of the nave and the dome.

It will be recalled that in the Great Model design Wren had provided for a deep western bay with a smaller but still substantial dome over it. In one way or another the idea of a western narthex or introductory bay to the nave persisted through all the various stages of design and what we see here is the result. Adjoining the north tower, it is expressed as an exceptionally deep bay divided vertically, as will be more fully described below, into three elements. The horizontal division into two storeys follows on from the west front, and the lower storey rests similarly on a base which is fully rusticated (i.e. the masonry is deeply scored to confirm the impression of being comprised of regularly-sized blocks). This base is interrupted below the tower by one of the magnificent doorways mentioned earlier, and interrupted again in the midde of the west bay of the nave by a low segmental-headed window which is one of the series lighting the crypt. (The crypt is unusual in extending beneath the entire building.)

The lower storey of this west bay was originally provided to be the Morning Chapel, and the upper storey is a room called the Trophy Room which used to contain the Great Model. It is normally inaccessible to members of the public. On the south side of the cathedral the equivalent room is the Library, with the former Consistory Court below. So far as the architecture is concerned, we are by now on familiar ground. Each stage is divided into three elements by pilasters, Corinthian below and Composite above, and the entablatures at two levels follow on from the west front once more. On the left or east side of the bay is a pair of pilasters, which give visual stability to that part of the composition—all such considerations having been very carefully weighed by Wren—and also help to balance the bay with the tower, which has pairs of pilasters at its corners both to define it and to give it visual strength.

The lower stage has a central round-headed window enriched by one of those vigorously-carved winged cherubs' heads supporting a scroll which are a special joy of St Paul's. On either side are niches with carved panels below and fielded panels above. The three frieze panels incorporate swags of flowers, ribbons and winged cherubs' heads all in daringly high relief. (All these sculptures are protected to some extent by the widely overhanging cornice above, and seem to be in remarkably good condition.)

The upper storey has a nicely balanced composition of three windows, the central one being like those in the ringing chamber of the tower and the side windows thinner and round-headed. Below all three are panels, bursting with carvings of ribbon, and swags of flowers.

Above we see for the first time the balustrade, which Wren did not want to add. The decision to add a balustrade above the blocking course was one taken at a very late stage by the Commissioners for building the new cathedral. Wren declared that such a balustrade would be 'contrary to the principles of good architecture', and took the opportunity to urge that statues should be erected on the pediments as in the best Greek and Roman architecture, 'the principles of which, throughout all my schemes of this colossal structure, I have religiously endeavoured to follow; and, if I glory, it is in the singular mercy of God, who has enabled me to begin and finish my great works so conformable to the ancient model.' However, in 1718 the Commissioners despatched one of their number, no less a person than Sir Isaac Newton, to discuss the matter with

Wren, and reluctantly, he gave in and selected one of the designs proposed by John James. The master mason employed for this job was Christopher Cass, who had worked at Blenheim Palace in Oxfordshire. The slight clumsiness of the junctions of the balustrade with the western towers and at the east end are some of the visual indications that it was added as an afterthought and not as part of Wren's own carefully considered original plans.

The Dome

This is also the first place from which to begin to take the measure of the dome. It rises visually from the beginnings of the north transept and the main north flank of the nave, the latter consisting of three bays in which the elements we have already noticed are largely carried on: a rusticated base with segmental-headed windows; a single enriched round-arched window in the lower storey; and in the upper storey a new arrangement in which an aedicule frames not a window but a niche and then below it, where one expects a panel of carved ornament to be, there is a segmental-headed window which lights the space above the north and south aisles of the nave.

The dome is closely integrated into all this, and not something existing in a separate sphere. Above the line of the nave balustrade rises a great masonry drum, stupendous in its simplicity and strength. Then comes the core of the design, a lofty stage in which a ring of colossal Corinthian columns supports the main entablature, above which is a balustrade which Wren evidently *did* intend. The columns are assisted in their task, structually and visually, by two compositional features. Firstly, at eight points round the circumference are solid-looking masonry in-fillings, ornamented by shell-headed niches with fielded panels and cherubs' heads and swags above; these are all in Ketton stone, from Rutland, a stone which has a distinctly golden-brown tinge, a deliberate instance of 'structural polychromy'. Secondly, the intervening columns are seen to have a short section of masonry walling attaching them to the inner wall, and these short sections are pierced by round-headed arches (a kind of triumphal arch motif) and above them roundels, with keystones.

Above the balustrade lies a zone full of movement achieved by differentiating each bay by blocked pilasters with projecting entablatures and by giving the window openings aprons over them which have little drops at either end. The effect is a rippling undulating movement, which is of the essence of the Baroque style. The windows, incidentally, are not windows at all but are openings filled with black marble, an example of Baroque illusionism and also of the colouristic use of different materials.

Then comes the dome itself, achieving a remarkable sense of harmony and repose. Lead-covered (and weathered to a supremely beautiful tonality), the segments are divided by prominent lead-covered rolls, and a double ring runs right round its base. Above it is the lantern, which seems more Neo-Classical than Baroque. The base is encircled by a viewing platform with gilded railings, supported on a stone base with scrolly brackets. The principal stage then consists of four identical frontispieces, facing the cardinal points, with pairs of coupled columns supporting an entablature and at the same time framing a rectangular window. On the cornice sit pairs of urns, over the columns. Then comes an attic stage with a *l'oeil de boeuf* window on all four sides, and a small dome with gilded ribs and 'portholes'. Above the dome rises the most famous feature of all, the immense gilded cross with floriated arms, supported on a huge gilded orb which is itself supported by a ring of scrolls. It is difficult to contemplate this climax of the building without feelings of exaltation and awe.

The visitor is recommended then to walk up into the middle of Paternoster Square, to obtain a broader and more distant view of the dome, a first look at the north transept and its group of fine figure sculptures, and the attractively contrasting north flank of the red-brick Chapter House. Here one can also see, looking away from St Paul's, a glimpse of Wren's fine tower to the church of Christ Church, Newgate Street, and enjoy Dame Elizabeth Frink's sculpture group of the *Good Shepherd and his sheep*.

The Chapter House

Returning close to the north side of the cathedral provides a good moment to enjoy the south façade of the Chapter House, built by Wren in 1711–14. It is a straightforward town palace, in effect, with three storeys—the middle one being a *piano nobile*, with larger windows, for the principal rooms—over a basement. Its red brick now comes as something of a shock (but a pleasant one) amongst so much stone, reminding us of such buildings as Kensington Palace (by Wren for William III and Mary II, 1689–96) and its Orangery (built under Nicholas

Hawksmoor's direction, 1704–5) and of Marlborough House (built, like Blenheim, for the first Duke of Marlborough, but by Wren, or more likely his son, 1709–11). The corners and the divisions between the bays are marked by rusticated pilasters, contrastingly in stone. The brick is predominantly mulberry colour, but the window surrounds and the aprons below the two upper rows of windows are in a more brightly-coloured brick. The original building was severely damaged in the Second World War, and the present building is a skilful recreation by the then Surveyor to the Fabric, W Godfrey Allen, in the late 1950s. Beneath visitors' feet, in the area between the Chapter House and the cathedral, lie the workshops of the specialist craftsmen whose unceasing programmes of conservation and repair keep the fabric of St Paul's in good order. There is a permanent work-force of skilled men, under the direction of a Clerk of Works, and under the ultimate supervision of a Surveyor to the Fabric, at present Professor William Whitfield.

The North Transept

Looking at the cathedral again, we perceive that in the angle between the nave and north transept is a projecting subsidiary element repeated in the other three equivalent angles. These house vestries at ground-floor level in three instances, and a staircase in the fourth. There are three tiers of rectangular windows and, at the angle, the outer of the two pairs of pilasters meet at a right angle. The lower frieze of ribbons and swags is carried on from the nave but here, as an added enrichment, there are similar carved panels for the upper order as well. This is a feature which is also repeated at the other four corners of the crossing. Visually and structurally these four corner towers (for such, in a sense, they are) help to support the great mass of the dome.

The remaining west-facing bay of the transept has the same articulation as the three main bays of the nave. The keystones of the small upper windows, here and on the nave, are carved with acanthus sprays which alternate with the Dean and Chapter's coat of arms framed also by acanthus. Unlike the corners of the intermediary staircase tower and the west bay of the nave, the external corners of the transept meet at a point and not at an inverted right angle. This is because the pilasters are set back from the edges of the rusticated masonry.

Before the Second World War there was a famous view of

the north transept from a narrow passageway opposite, which enabled one to see a thin slice of the building from the ground to the top of the cross. The foot of the present Cathedral Steps is still an excellent place from which to view and absorb the majestic frontispiece to the transept. Put briefly, there is again a division into three bays, in two storeys, and the side bays are of the standard form. The whole transept is made arresting and monumental, however, by Wren's use of a broad central pediment at the top and by the boldly projecting semi-circular portico to the lower stage. This is such a striking motif that we at once want to know its origins. Wren would have known well (from engravings, since he never went to Rome) the entrance portico of Pietro da Cortona's church of Sta Maria della Pace, in Rome (1656–7). The same motif was used a little later on by Thomas Archer at St Paul, Deptford (1717–30), and by James Gibbs at St Mary-le-Strand (1714–17). Both churches were built for the Commissioners for Building Fifty New Churches in London or the Suburbs Thereof; Wren and Archer were fellow Commissioners, and Gibbs (for a time) was one of the two Surveyors.

Within the portico is the north doorway; and over it a projecting panel of plain masonry (contrasting with the rusticated masonry at the sides) which raises the exuberantly carved frieze upwards and to a climax in the centre with a garlanded urn: a truly festive concept, with a Baroque element of swagger and display. Over the portico is a large segmental-headed window of a type (with 'ears' to the architrave or frame) which derives from French Baroque examples.

The pilasters framing the central window are carved with swags of flowers, fruit and leaves for their whole length, like the even more magnificent ones in the library. The keystone of the window is another winged cherub's head, in fronds of foliage. The side bays are simpler, by contrast: round-headed niches are the principal features, with square fielded panels above them.

Within the pediment is the Royal Arms of William III, supported by full-length figures of angels, and by a seated lion and unicorn. The sculptor was Grinling Gibbons.

The pediment and the two corners of the transept are crowned by five more figures of apostles by Francis Bird (there

The semi-circular portico of the north transept, influenced by Pietro da Cortona's Sta Maria della Pace in Rome.

are five others on the south transept, and St Peter and St James
flank St Paul on the west front).

The Churchyard

The northern perimeter of St Paul's churchyard is bordered by
iron railings; originally these ran all the way round, and they
still encircle the southern perimeter. Wren had at first proposed a wrought-iron fence round the churchyard, by the
master ironsmith Thomas Robinson. From 1707, however,
Wren had to face a hostile Building Committee under Dean
Godolphin; and this Committee insisted upon a cast-iron fence
(which is what we see) by Richard Jones, described by Jane
Lang (p. 248) as 'a workman of shady reputation whose
proposals Wren considered ugly, extravagant, and quite un-
suitable'. Nevertheless, these same railings, which cost
£11,700, are now highly valued as some of the earliest cast-
iron we possess, and the long run along the north side of the
churchyard is undoubtedly impressive.

The churchyard is beautifully planted, chiefly with plane
trees and ground-cover shrubs, and there are some scattered
tombs; but the most prominent feature is the present Paul's
Cross, designed by Sir Reginald Blomfield in 1906 with
sculpture by Sir Bertram Mackennal. Originally Paul's Cross
was an outdoor pulpit, and both before and after the Reforma-
tion it was a prominent feature of life in the City of London
until the Great Fire of 1666. It is not known what the earliest
form of Paul's Cross was like, but Bishop Kempe gave a new
one in 1449 and in the post-Reformation period there was a
Jacobean one. Proposals to replace it and to revive the tradition
of outdoor preaching came to nothing for more than two
hundred years, and it must be admitted that the present one—
though a very agreeable piece of design—is not in the least like
a pulpit. It takes the form of a Tuscan column, on which stands
a sculpture of St Paul. Angelic boys playing with wreaths
support the foot of the column, raised over a base with scrolly
volutes at the corners; all this is enclosed within a retaining wall
which is presumably the 'pulpit'. What Mr H C Richards, who
had left £5,000 in his will 'to rebuild Paul's Cross', would have
thought of it is unclear. But in 1910 Canon Scott Holland
wrote to Blomfield that 'It is the most beautiful and appropriate monument in London. The figure at the top has a touch of
importance about it, and the boys round the base are delicious.
I think the entire monument explains itself, and looks entirely

An eighteenth-century engraving of St Paul's, showing the relationship of the east end to the dome and transepts.

at home in its position.' One can understand from this that the new Paul's Cross was to be rather a 'memorial' to its predecessors than an attempt to recreate one of them (though the latter is probably what the donor hoped for). The site of the former Paul's Cross is closer to the cathedral, and is marked on the ground by an inscription.

The Choir

The north wall of the choir rises like a backdrop to the churchyard. It continues the pattern established by the nave for three bays, and then there is a further but shorter east bay with a plain niche under a flat architrave in the upper zone, and a shell-headed and more attenuated niche in the lower zone with other ornamental features. The frieze, for instance, has a small circular opening with a carved border, and a heavy swag below it. There is additional carved ornament above and below the architrave of the niche and further below a deliciously carved porthole window with a shelly surround, like something from a grotto.

The East End

Arriving at the east end of the building, the central curved apse (echoed by the transept porticoes), is framed by a bay on either side with pairs of pilasters at the outer edges. It is interesting to see what happens next. First there is a half-pilaster, at both levels, which is the final framing of the side bays, and becomes the first element of the apse. Second, while the usual forms continue at the lower level, at the upper level there is an astonishing and climactic transformation ('transformation' is a key element in Baroque architecture). The outer wall surface as it were dissolves, and instead of a window we have a triumphal arch pierced through the wall; beyond is an inner window with carved keystone and spandrels and further ornament in the head of the inner arch. The ceiling is coffered, and all is richness and dynamic power. The keystone of the outer arch is carved with acanthus leaf, and over it is the central feature of the frieze, an incense-pot or censer (rather than an urn). The holy of holies has been reached; through its ornament and form the building expresses its high purpose eloquently.

The pilasters are also, at the upper level, transformed into engaged columns, and above the centre bay rises an attic storey which melts away at the sides into flattened volutes. The central feature of the attic stage is a circular window wreathed in acanthus leaves which lights the roof space.

At this point the visitor has to skirt the new buildings of St Paul's Choir School. They are by Leo de Syllas of Architects' Co-Partnership, 1962–7, and incorporate the restored tower and spectacular steeple of Wren's church of St Augustine, Watling Street (1695; altered in *c.* 1860, damaged in the War and the steeple recreated in 1967 according to the original profile by Seely and Paget). An admirable view of the whole ensemble can be had from the Memorial Gardens to the south-east of the cathedral on the site of the former medieval street of Old Change. In this area of the medieval precincts was the famous St Paul's School, founded by Dean Colet in 1512.

Further south-east is the red brick and sandstone office block of the *Financial Times* newspaper, Bracken House, a fine building designed in 1956–9 by Sir Albert Richardson, who is commemorated in the crypt of St Paul's.

At the west end of the formal garden is a bronze sculpture, *The Young Lovers*, by Georg Ehrlich (1897–1966). The combination of stone walls, grass, water, pleached lime trees, and

The pelican wounding its breast to feed its young, architectural carving towards the east end of St Paul's, 1690s.

sculpture is extremely pleasing; and this is certainly one of the best places from which to enjoy the cathedral.

Having reached the south side of the cathedral we are hardly surprised to find that it closely mirrors the north side. Regrettably, the south flank of the building, more exposed to traffic, has become much dirtier than the north since the great stone-cleaning programme initiated in 1958. Similarly, the pairs of specially fine urns on garlanded columns flanking the south transept have recently had to be replaced by new ones. These, like the originals, are of Portland stone carved by the cathedral's own craftsmen.

The South Transept

In the pediment of the south transept, in the position where the Royal Arms appears on the north side, is a phoenix (symbol of resurrection) with the single word RESURGAM (Latin, meaning 'I shall rise again'). This was carved by Cibber, and recalls an incident reported in *Parentalia* (see p. 43).

The curious visitor may notice in the churchyard on the south side of the choir a low pedimented stone structure, which is the entrance to the former St Gregory's parochial burial vault. Of greater interest are the indications, laid out in the grass on the south side of the nave, of the former medieval Chapter House and cloister. Between them is a bronze

sculpture by Bainbridge Copnall, placed here by the Corporation of London in 1973, which appears to represent St Paul at
the moment of Conversion. Unexpectedly it is labelled 'Beck-
ett'. St Thomas à Becket was born nearby in Cheapside.

Passing the west bay of the nave we notice that two of the
carved panels below the niches are carved with motifs which
include books, a reference to the Dean and Chapter's library on
the first floor above. Then there is the Dean's Door in the
tower, leading to the Geometrical Staircase, which we shall see
within.

The Deanery

From here it is an easy step to cross the road into Dean's Court,
to see the Old Deanery. This was most probably designed
either by John Oliver or by Wren's first deputy at St Paul's,
Edward Woodroffe, who signed the contract for the house on
behalf of Dean Sancroft in 1672. Like the Chapter House, it is
built of two contrasting-coloured bricks. It is a handsome
seven-bay house with a hipped roof and a pretty cobbled
courtyard. Now used as offices, it was superbly restored (from
a state of near dereliction) in 1981–2 by Haslemere Estates.
Next to it is the former Choir School, now a much frequented
Youth Hostel, built by F C Penrose in 1875 in an Italian
Renaissance style. It has two storeys with an attic, the upper
storey faced with glazed bricks and the lower with yellow
London stock bricks: a curious mixture. Curious also, but
endearing, is the window on the corner by the Deanery; and
there is a Latin inscription in red sgraffito lettering between the
ground and upper floors.

Amen Court

To complete an exploration of the buildings in the immediate
ambit of St Paul's, cross the main road again and walk
westwards a short distance, turning right into Ave Maria Lane.
Here is a link with the medieval precincts again, if only in the
name; and shortly, on the left, you can enter Amen Court with
its row of houses for members of the Chapter built by Edward
Woodroffe in 1670. In the nineteenth century this enclave was
enlarged, and the north side of the inner courtyard in red brick
and terracotta looks and feels like a quadrangle in one of the
smaller Oxford or Cambridge colleges. These additional
houses were designed by Ewan Christian, architect to the
Ecclesiastical Commissioners, in 1880.

Chapter Four

AN ARCHITECTURAL WALK ROUND THE INTERIOR OF ST PAUL'S

Nave, Aisles and Western Chapels

On entering by either of the double-leaved original doors set towards the north and south sides of the great west front, the visitor experiences a thrilling vista along the north or south aisle to the very east end of the cathedral. He finds himself in a spacious stone lobby with a doorway on one side and a niche beautifully balancing it on the other. Pausing to take in the character and nature of the architecture, it will be noticed that the barrel vault and the side walls are broken down into three elements. The side walls are articulated by giant pilasters of the Composite order (that is, their capitals combine the scrolly volutes of the Ionic order with the stylized acanthus leaves of the Corinthian order), which provide vertical emphasis and division; horizontal emphasis and division are provided by a frieze with carving of scrolls and flowers. The doorway (in the north vestibule leading to the Chapel of All Souls and in the south vestibule to the Dean's Staircase) and the niche give emphasis to the centre bay on either side; above and flanking these central elements are sunken panels. This introduces a characteristic aspect of St Paul's Baroque architecture, so noticeable also in the parish churches of Wren and in the work of his pupil Nicholas Hawksmoor: the wall surface is experienced as a series of layers or varying planes, of which the

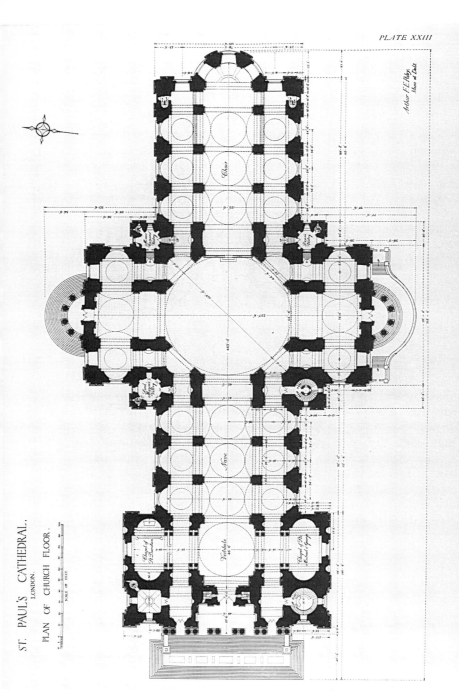

PLATE XXIII

Plan of the principal floor level of St Paul's from Arthur Poley's St Paul's Cathedral, London *(1932).*

pilasters represent the outermost layer and the fielded panels the innermost.

The central panel of the vault is plain, save for a moulded rectangular frame and two pairs of winged cherubs' heads, while the side panels are coffered in alternating layers of one long and two short divisions. This system of decoration was taken by architects of the Renaissance and Baroque periods from the architecture of Classical antiquity. A rich frieze of swags of fruit and flowers, ribbons, and the arms of the Dean and Chapter of St Paul's completes the ensemble.

At the east end of each vestibule is a short linking-passage, in which the wall surfaces are articulated by niches squeezed between a pair of pilasters to the west and a single pilaster to the east. Again, the heads of the niches are ornamented with rich carving, and the vault is coffered.

Looking down the aisle, the visitor notices that—with appropriate variations—the ordinance of the architecture and the vocabulary of the carved ornament follow the general pattern which has already been observed and commented upon. For example, the vaults of the aisles alternate between coffered and panelled sections like the linking-passages from the vestibules and, over the bays themselves, are set the plastered white surfaces of shallow domes, each of which is framed by a sumptuously carved band of stone. The western bays of the aisles, which are longer than the rest and border the western chapels, have transverse barrel vaults within which are set rectangular frames with curved ends. The other three bays, on each side, are uniform and it is necessary only to draw attention to the elevations and the way in which the windows are framed: the essential point is that each bay is like a shallow concave apse, scalloped out of the thickness of the wall. In each bay is placed a round-headed window, centrally, with alternating patterns of rich coffering over. On either side of the window the wall is again treated with sunken panels, which gives a richness to the surface; and below the window is a carved frieze of stylized flower and leaf motifs combined with strapwork. The panels in the concave space below the frieze have in most cases been filled with sculptured monuments.

The differentiation of the western bay of the nave from the other three bays is one of the most striking features of the building and one which survived from Wren's earlier designs. It has a number of consequences for the architecture and, first and foremost, it means that after the constriction of the vestibules and linking-passages one emerges into a wide, lofty and spectacular space, approximately square in plan, which has few equals in English architecture for its nobility and grandeur. The halls at Blenheim Palace, Oxfordshire, and Castle Howard, Yorkshire, are perhaps the nearest parellels and, in both those cases, while the overall designer was Sir John Vanbrugh, the assistance of Nicholas Hawksmoor, who worked as Wren's assistant at St Paul's cathedral from *c.* 1684 onwards, is regarded as having been crucial.

Looking at this west bay in some detail, one notices for the first time the use of two of the Classical orders in a way which thereafter becomes normative throughout the building. The lower order, as in the vestibules, is Composite; by contrast the giant order, whose pilasters are fluted, is a sumptuous Corinthian in which the acanthus leaves are wonderfully deeply undercut. As in the three main bays of the nave the side walls are, of course, pierced to the aisles; but added weight, dignity and splendour is given here by supporting the arches on pairs of coupled columns, square and circular respectively, which introduces the Palladian 'Venetian window' motif of a semi-circular-headed arch between two flat-headed elements. The same compositional format is used for the arches into the side chapels—that on the north is now St Dunstan's Chapel but was originally a Morning Chapel, used for morning prayer, while that on the south is the Chapel of the Order of St Michael and St George, but was originally set out as the Consistory Court of the diocese. This grouping of inner and outer layers of coupled columns greatly increases the impression of depth at the sides of the western bay and provides a succession of spaces framing and supporting the centre. The chapels, with their spectacular carved wooden screens by Jonathan Maine, are only open on application; but from the western bay of the nave one can see that they are square vaulted spaces given extra length by eastern and western apses with radiating coffering. The vault of the Chapel of the Order of St Michael and St George is more richly ornamented than that of St Dunstan's Chapel, as the four octagonal panels are carved with heraldry and foliage dating from 1906. The vault of the Chapel of St Michael and St George is also gilded.

A few other aspects of the western bay deserve notice. The west doorway, opened on occasions like the reception of a new dean or bishop or the wedding of the Prince and Princess of Wales, is on a heroic scale. The western internal elevation evokes another important precedent from antiquity, the triumphal arch. The stone vault over the entrance bay peels back in several layers, with bands of guilloche ornament and coffering leading the eye inwards and onwards towards the west window. Within the deeply recessed lunette shapes set high up over the three closed sides of the western bay are placed rectangular windows; these are framed by vertical panels which contain carving of quite exceptional quality (though difficult to see from the floor of the nave, and at the time of writing in need of cleaning). The great circlet of stone framing the shallow saucer dome is substantially deeper and more richly carved than those over the three main bays of the nave. Framing the side arches is an arrangement of ornamental detailing which deserves particular attention. Over the paired columns, on either side, are square-headed niches containing elaborate ornamental obelisks on stands. Below these are swags with fronds carved with breath-taking virtuosity, and above them are carved cartouches, all four of them miracles of design and execution. Finally, although the full entablature running across the west wall cannot be continued across the arches north and south because of their height, the prominently projecting cornice not only runs round all three sides of the western bay but is a vital unifying feature of the whole interior architecture.

It remains only to describe the central vessel of the nave. As has already been noticed, this consists principally of three great bays pierced with arches through to the aisles, plus an eastern bay, a little shorter than the rest, which is contained within two of the massive piers supporting the dome. There is a marvellous serenity in the rhythmic progression of one bay to another, and in the telling contrast between the whitened surfaces of the domes over the bays of nave and aisles and the brownish-grey tonality of the stonework.

The arrangement of each of these three main bays is as follows. The arches are taller than in the western bay, and fill the whole space available supported on an inner Composite order of square columns. Each arch is coffered, and over it on the nave side is a triplet of winged *putti* or cherubs. Over the cornice, here and throughout the building, runs a stone gallery with railings of gilt metal. The railing of the west gallery was designed and made in the workshops of the great French artist-blacksmith Jean Tijou *c.* 1708, and his rail is continued along the north and south galleries as far as the entrances to the rooms on either side of the western bay of the nave. The rail was continued, in closely matching work, only in the nineteenth century under the direction of Francis Penrose, whose long reign as Surveyor to the Fabric extended from 1852 to 1897. After the virtuoso stone carving, the metalwork is the second of the three chief aesthetic pleasures of St Paul's (the third is the no less virtuoso woodcarving, especially in the choir stalls, the screens and in the library) and the western bay provides our introduction to it. The robust, spiky wrought-iron railings to the north and south chapels were executed *c*. 1698 by Thomas Robinson, one of several English blacksmiths who worked for Wren at St Paul's, a member of the small army of excellent craftsmen whom he had a genius for finding and who did some of their best work for him.

Above the level of the stone gallery on either side the vault begins to spring. Between the bays are bands of stone with double bands of guilloche ornament. These, and the circlets of stone framing the shallow saucer domes, are the principal enrichments of the vault. Between the domes and the vertical side walls are carved segmental areas richly carved with a laurel wreath in the centre flanked by floriated ornament. At this upper clerestory level is a large segmental-headed window in each bay, more conventionally Baroque than those in the western bay; the frames have inner and outer bands of ornament, lobed corners at the top, a console placed centrally over the arch to give emphasis, and flat curling volutes at the sides. Between each bay is a single fluted Corinthian pilaster of the giant order, dissolving into coupled pilasters only at the east and west ends of the main spaces of the nave.

The eastern bay follows the overall ordinance of the higher and lower zones, but there are many subtle differences dictated by the existence of solid walls instead of arches. The frieze of the lower order is carried round to the inner walls, and below it on each side is a sunken panel supported on the south side by a projecting bracket on volutes. In this bay the entablature reappears, another link with the west wall of the nave. The vault has the most developed form of coffering (compare this example with that over the windows of the aisles), in which the outer bordered rectangle encloses a smaller bordered rectangle, enclosing in its turn a large stylized flower. The whole is further enriched by gilding.

The Dome and Transepts

This is the heart of the building, and the place above all to pause and contemplate the scale and richness of the architecture. It is not easy, simply by looking at the building at this point, to work out exactly how the structural systems work and how the different elements support one another.

The first thing to note is that the area is divided into two distinct zones, the upper one being the dome itself, and the lower one consisting of eight arches supported on eight nearly rectangular piers which extend back into the nave, transepts and choir and which form the inner bays of those parts of the building. Four of the arches reach from floor to coffered vault, while the four intermediary arches enclose complex architectural compositions which form, as it were, screens across four massive corner piers which serve as an outer ring of support for the massive weight of the dome. What is actually seen of these outer piers is one diagonal corner and two side walls articulated by the lower order of Composite pilasters, and arches linking the outer piers with the inner ring of eight piers. These arches form part of the vault of eight linking-passages returning to the aisles of nave, transept and choir. The giant order of the inner ring in turn supports a single taller arch which encloses a semi-dome decorated, in the nineteenth century, with mosaic. This arch interrupts the stone gallery and its railing, but above the semi-dome is an alternative recessed gallery with its own semi-dome and transverse arches. Attention must be called to the rich carving of the cartouches and their swags of flowers on the diagonal corners of the outer piers.

Between the eight giant arches are spandrels, now also filled with mosaics, and above them the great projecting cornice with its Tijou railing, known as the 'Whispering Gallery' (access is from the door at the east end of the south aisle), on account of its remarkable acoustical properties.

Then begins the drum of the dome. First there is a deep blank stage of plain masonry; then a richly carved and gilded frieze; and finally the stage which is punctuated by pilasters of the Composite order, and in which there is a rhythm of three windows followed by a niche so that the division below into eight arched bays is reflected by what happens above. The niches, whether or not Wren intended them to be filled, remained empty until 1892–4 when they were given colossal sculptures of the Fathers of the Church designed by C E Kempe and made by Frederick Winnington of the firm of

Farmer and Brindley. (C E Kempe was better known for the stained glass produced by his own firm. It is difficult to imagine, when experiencing the cathedral today flooded by sunshine, that until the time of the Second World War its windows were filled with much stained glass of the nineteenth and early twentieth centuries.) The pilasters support another circular entablature, above which rises the inner dome with its paintings by Sir James Thornhill, 1716–19. At this point it is necessary to recall that, as explained in the section on the *Evolution of the Design of St Paul's* in Chapter Two, St Paul's has not one dome but three. What one sees from the outside is the lead-covered outer dome on a wooden framework. What one sees from the floor of the cathedral is the innermost painted dome and its upper gallery, through which can be glimpsed a further, painted upper dome whose central rosette is pierced to allow the eye to penetrate even further, to the inside of the lantern. The upper dome is part of a great cone of brickwork, otherwise concealed from view, which rises between the inner and outer layers and which supports the massive weight of the crowning glory of the stone lantern, and also the wooden framework for the outer lead dome. The paintings of the inner dome are described in the chapter on the Furnishings and Works of Art.

The architecture of the transepts, which balance one another closely, comprises elements already encountered in the nave. Once again there is an upper and a lower zone. The lower zone continues the order of giant Corinthian pilasters at one level and the Composite order at a lower level, and the outer walls are given a rich surface appearance by the friezes of the upper and lower orders and by the three panels of ornament (candlesticks and swags) between the upper and the lower friezes. In the centre bay of each wall is a lofty double-leaved door within a doorway of monumental scale (that in the south transept being interrupted by a porch-gallery placed here in the nineteenth century but made up of seventeenth-century woodwork from the original pulpitum). In the upper zone, over each doorway, is a tall window treated in the same way as those in the western bay of the nave. The elevations are like those of the two eastern bays of the nave, i.e. there is a shorter inner bay dictated as to many of its characteristics by the existence of the inner ring of piers, and then an outer bay which is like one of the three principle bays of the nave. The vault is treated in the same way, i.e. coffered and surmounted by a shallow saucer dome. Between the dome and the side walls on the east and west sides are the same curved segmental areas with carved wreaths and panels of ornament. The north transept vault, and the upper part of the north wall, suffered extensive damage in the Second World War. It is of particular interest to note the high quality of the post-war replacement carving, which can be distinguished from the original work by its lighter colour.

The Choir, Aisles and Eastern Chapels

Among the many enjoyable characteristics of St Paul's are the balance and repose of its architecture, and the relationships between the different parts of the building. The Classical repose of the architecture lives side by side with the exuberant richness of the detailing of the building and its lavish Baroque sculpture. The choir is related to the nave by being virtually the latter in reverse, except that its climax is the eastern apse rather than a great square space.

The first choir bay, whose side walls are dominated by the organ cases placed here in the nineteenth century, is essentially the same as the eastern bay of the nave, with the same bands of guilloche ornament framing a coffered barrel vault. In the whole of the eastern arm, the gilding has been brought up to a high pitch of splendour in order that the architectural ornament and the late nineteenth-century mosaics (described later) may form one integrated scheme of decoration. It must be said that the mosaics seem to fit the character of the architecture well, but one might well ask what Wren's original intentions were. We have a clue, in a footnote on p. 292 of *Parentalia*: this deals at some length with the question of interior decoration and finish, and since it is one of the most important passages in the authentic literature relating to this subject, it is worth recapitulating what it says. First of all it refers to the dome, where instead of the Thornhill paintings Wren intended 'to have beautified the Inside of the Cupola with the more durable Ornament of Mosaick-work, as is nobly executed in the Cupola of St Peter's in Rome, which strikes the Eye of the Beholder with a most magnificent and splendid Appearance; and which, without the least Decay of Colours, is as lasting as Marble, or the Building itself'. Then it refers to the decoration of the choir and hints at the proposal for a great baldacchino over the altar: 'The Painting and Gilding of the Architecture of the East-end of the Church over the Communion Table was intended only to serve the present Occasion, till such Time as Materials could have been procured for a magnificent Design of an Altar, consisting of four Pillars wreathed, of the richest Greek Marbles, supporting a Canopy hemispherical, with proper Decorations of Architecture and Sculpture: for which the respective Drawings, and a Model were prepared.' The provisional 'Painting and Gilding' referred to must have been, in its way, magnificent in its effect. The stonework of the apse had been painted to make it resemble marble; the four great fluted pilasters supporting the main entablature were coloured ultramarine veined with gold to resemble lapis lazuli; the capitals of the pilasters and the carved mouldings of the entablature were gilded; details were picked out, to give the carving an additional resonance and richness; and a golden glory was painted on the stonework of the vault above the upper range of windows. The curved wall of the apse was lined with a framework of gilded wood within which were set twenty-one panels of flowered crimson velvet. All this was the backdrop for the Communion table or altar itself, a table of great beauty made by the master joiner William Samwell and now used as the altar of the Lady Chapel in the south choir aisle. It stood originally on a Persian carpet, and over it was placed a fringed altarcloth of crimson velvet, patterned with gold lace; on it were placed a pair of fine gold candlesticks, and copies of the Bible and the Book of Common Prayer in covers of chased gold resting on velvet cushions.

After the three principal bays of the choir, and their vaults, there follows a final short bay, essentially the same as the organ bay but with the entablature being taken up again, leading to the three-sided apse. Seen from the west, the apse is interrupted by the baldacchino designed after the Second World War by Stephen Dykes Bower in collaboration with the then Surveyor to the Fabric, W Godfrey Allen. This provides exactly the right sense of exalted climax to the building, quite apart from being an astonishing artistic achievement of our own time. As we have seen in the quotation above ('an Altar, consisting of four Pillars wreathed . . . supporting a Canopy hemispherical') Wren clearly intended something of this kind, if the money, materials and support had been forthcoming.

Behind and above the baldacchino the giant order with its fluted pilasters continues round the apse, and there are three round-headed windows at the upper level and three at the lower. All these windows are filled with glass by Brian

The climax of the building: the vaults of the choir are covered with Richmond's mosaics of the 1890s, and dramatically sited in front of the apse is the baldacchino by Stephen Dykes Bower (1958).

Thomas, nicely judged—with their predominant blues and golds—to play their part in the overall scheme of things. The mosaics, too, rise to their own visual climax in the apse with Christ the Ruler of All Things in the central panel, flanked by cherubim with strong, pre-Raphaelite faces.

The choir aisles are, as we would expect, also like those of the nave. The west bay is like the east bay of the nave aisles, and also like the western vestibules, in that the architecture is similarly composed and articulated with a doorway on one side and a niche on the other. The doorways lead to vestries, themselves magnificent small late seventeenth-century rooms; on the north is the Minor Canons' Vestry and on the south the Dean's Vestry. (The corresponding spaces off the east bay of the nave aisles are occupied by the Lord Mayor's Vestry on the north and the circular staircase to the gallery of the dome on the south.)

Then there follow three principal bays, pierced with arches to the central vessel of the choir, and a final short bay terminating not in a smaller version of the central apse but in a flat wall in which is deeply set the round-headed window, with plain glazing, which can be seen on first entering the building.

Although the choir aisles are architecturally so similar to those of the nave they feel quite different. This is partly because they are closed, on their inner sides, by the backs of the choir stalls, and partly because their vaults are encrusted with mosaics and gilding like the choir itself. In the north choir aisle is the *Mother and Child* sculpture by Henry Moore CH, by universal acclaim the greatest British sculptor of the twentieth century, which he gave to the cathedral and for this site in 1984; two former organ consoles repose here also, somewhat inconsequentially. The east end of this aisle is designated as the Modern Martyrs' Chapel, to commemorate those Anglican Christians who have died for their faith since 1850. It is a most imaginative idea though, as yet, its furnishing and decoration are not equal to its great theme. A small sanctuary contains a panelled wooden altar, and over it is a marble sculpture from the late nineteenth-century high altar reredos of Christ on the Cross.

The east end of the south aisle is furnished as a Lady Chapel. One special adornment is the *Mary and the Child Jesus* sculpture which, before it was damaged during the Second World War, formed an important part of the former lofty high altar reredos, designed by G F Bodley, one of the greatest English Gothicists of the late nineteenth century, and carved by the firm of Farmer and Brindley. Another particular treasure is Wren's original late seventeenth-century Communion table, referred to earlier in the description of its original setting. On the altar table now is a pair of Rococo wooden candlesticks and a cross, *en suite*, originating in southern Germany in the eighteenth century and given to St Paul's by the West German nation after the Second World War. By such admirable gestures are relationships rebuilt.

The apse itself, behind the baldacchino which shelters the high altar, is furnished as the American Memorial Chapel, dedicated on 26 November 1958, in memory of those Americans who gave their lives in the Second World War. Artistically this is a great success, including the floor of black and white marble with its radiating patterns, the crystal chandeliers, the altar with its cloth of rich red velvet embroidered in

OPPOSITE: Looking west from the American Chapel in the apse. The glass case in the foreground contains a book which records the names of 28,000 American servicemen and women who died in the Second World War. The high altar beind by Stephen Dykes Bower is of Italian marble.

THIS CHAPEL COMMEMORATES THE COMMON SACRIFICES OF
THE BRITISH AND AMERICAN PEOPLES DURING THE SECOND
WORLD WAR AND ESPECIALLY THOSE AMERICAN SERVICE MEN
WHOSE NAMES ARE RECORDED IN ITS ROLL OF HONOUR
THIS TABLET WAS UNVEILED BY H.M. QUEEN ELIZABETH II
ON 26 NOVEMBER 1958 IN THE PRESENCE OF RICHARD M. NIXON
THE VICE PRESIDENT OF THE UNITED STATES OF AMERICA

gold recalling the original covering of Wren's altar in the 1690s, the cross and candlesticks, and the richly carved and gilded reredos and flanking curved stalls. Specially to be admired are the vertical strips of carving: they are a perfectly credible attempt to carve in the spirit of Grinling Gibbons without actually imitating him, and they were made by George Haslop.

From here too Brian Thomas's lower tier of windows can be enjoyed. Opposite the semi-circular sanctuary, which is enclosed by Communion rails in the style of Jean Tijou, is a gilded and glazed casket containing a Book of Remembance recalling all those whom the chapel commemorates.

The Crypt

The public entrance to the crypt is in the linking-passage in the east aisle of the south transept, and on descending its stone staircase the visitor is advised to turn right. Here begins the *Tour of the Monuments* (see p. 127) and also the south choir aisle of the crypt. The plan of the crypt is virtually the same as the main floor of the cathedral, but since some parts are inaccessible and there are also many points where a through view is impossible, the first impression tends to be rather confusing. Simply to enjoy the architectural spaces of the crypt there are three principal vantage points from which to make observations: towards the west end of the eastern arm (reached by turning left from the south choir aisle), the space under the dome, and the centre part of the nave.

From the first vantage point one can clearly see how the different elements in the crypt relate to one another and to the architecture above. The large square blocks of masonry to left and right support the piers of the choir arcades in the church above. In the crypt there is then an inner aisle with free-standing columns supporting a groined vault. The greater part of the eastern arm is laid out as the Chapel of the Most Excellent Order of the British Empire, with furnishings at the east end designed by Lord Mottistone and Paul Paget (who were successively Surveyors to the Fabric), and more glass by Brian Thomas. These are described elsewhere. In recent years the whole crypt has been whitened and re-lit, which has unified it visually and revealed it as a most enjoyable series of spaces.

West of the Chapel the two western bays of the eastern arm, contained within the two massive blocks of masonry which support the bays with the organ cases upstairs, are set apart to form a mausoleum for the sarcophagus and remains of the first Duke of Wellington and to commemorate the pre-eminent military commanders on the allied side who were Field Marshals in the Second World War.

West of that is an aisle, and west again through the outer ring of piers is the central space beneath the dome. It was a stroke of genius to place here, in an elegant Renaissance sarcophagus originally intended for the remains of Cardinal Wolsey in the sixteenth century, the remains of Admiral Lord Nelson. This is the pivotal point of the crypt and, with its inner circle of columns and central ring with wide flat ribs, it is visually an exciting place. To the north and south are the 'transepts', that on the north housing an enterprising Treasury with magnificent 'spider's web' gates in mild steel by Alan Evans, a Gloucestershire craftsman chosen after a limited competition organized by the Dean and Chapter and the Crafts Council in 1981.

West of the central space is another aisle, and then the nave and aisles of the crypt. Magnificently sited here, by another recent stroke of genius, is Wren's Great Model, described elsewhere (p. 39).

The Dean's Stair

In our perambulation of the exterior of the cathedral we have already noticed the ceremonial Dean's Doorway at the foot of the south-west tower (p. 68). Behind this door, and within the tower space itself, the master mason William Kempster and the artist-blacksmith Jean Tijou created one of the outstanding visual triumphs of St Paul's, the Dean's Stair (built 1703–5). The floor of the tower is paved with stone and black marble in a large star pattern. A stone handrail curves up to the level of the church floor, where a landing is given the most lavish treatment possible with a niche, garlands, cherub's head, scrolls of 'leatherwork', and a riotously inventive ironwork screen by Tijou. The remainder of the Geometrical Staircase (as it is also known) then curves upwards in an unbroken spiral to the doors at upper level giving access to the library and to the galleries of the nave. Each stone step is cantilevered: one end is set into the masonry of the wall and the other is supported by the step beneath it. English precedents for this were the stone staircase by Inigo Jones at The Queen's House, Greenwich (probably 1630–5), which Wren certainly would have known;

and a cantilevered staircase of walnut-wood at Drayton House, Northamptonshire, carried out in the time of the second Earl of Peterborough (d. 1697).

The Library

This room, which is over the Chapel of St Michael and St George and matched by a similar room (known variously as the Model Room or the Trophy Room but probably intended originally to be another library room) over St Dunstan's Chapel, is one of Wren's noblest spaces and without doubt one of the most magnificent and least-known rooms of its date in England. It was architecturally complete in the summer of 1704, when it was given a vaulted ceiling of brick covered over with cockleshell lime plaster of exceptionally high quality. Its fitting out was undertaken three years later. It is rectangular in shape, and the ceiling is deeply coved—almost a dome—and supported on four monumental stone arches. The long north and south sides are each divided into five bays by four square pilasters and on the fronts of these pilasters is some of the most wonderful stone carving in the whole cathedral. The lofty vertical swags show the tools of scholarship appropriate to a library—beautifully bound books, manuscripts, and quill pens—interspersed with flowers, fruit and ears of wheat. At the tops of the east and west pilasters on either side the scrolls bear the leaves of books, depicted with incredible virtuosity. The other four pilasters terminate in crowns or, in one case, a mitre. On the south side one of the pilasters shows a medieval bishop on a pilgrim's badge (presumably a reference to St Erkenwald) and another shows an hour-glass, emblem of mortality.

The second most notable feature of this astonishing room is the gallery running round all four sides, to provide upper and lower tiers of bookcases. Bay by bay the gallery is supported on thirty-two openwork scrolly brackets of wood carved by the master-carver Jonathan Maine; once again, these are amongst the most marvellous works of craftmanship in the entire cathedral. Their delicacy and openness makes it seem unlikely that they were ever particularly effective in carrying the weight of the gallery, which slopes alarmingly.

At the east end of the library is a handsome fireplace by the master mason Samuel Fulkes; it has a white marble surround with bolection moulding, and above it is a portrait of Bishop

OPPOSITE: The Dean's Stair.

The library, looking east.

William Nicholas (d. 1713). Above, the gallery carries the
Royal Arms of Queen Anne within a deliciously carved
cartouche. On the gallery front at the west end is a portrait of
Dr John Tillotson (dated 1687), who was a residentiary canon

of St Paul's while it was being built, was later Dean of St Paul's, and eventually Archbishop of Canterbury.

The present collection of books was started in 1707, when the Dean and Chapter were able to acquire a large number of books from the library of the late Revd Walter Gery, Vicar of Islington. A wagon drawn by five horses took two and a half days to bring all the books from Islington to St Paul's. Then the library received a magnificent bequest from Bishop Henry Compton, who died on 7 July 1713 (the day of a Thanksgiving for the Peace of Utrecht) after having been Bishop of London throughout the building of the cathedral. He left the Dean and Chapter 1,892 volumes. Partly by gift and partly by purchase, the books of Dr Thomas Mangey, Prebendary of Durham, and of his son, the Revd John Mangey, Prebendary of St Paul's, were acquired in 1783. In 1893 the Revd W Sparrow Simpson, who was sub-dean and librarian and a considerable collector, published a Catalogue of Bibles, Rituals, and Rare Books in the library of St Paul's, and included also works relating specially to the cathedral itself and the large collection of Paul's Cross sermons, maps, plans, and views of London and of St Paul's. Much material relating to St Paul's has in recent years been deposited in the Guildhall Library, where it has been catalogued.

The library contains other treasures besides books and manuscripts, including a delightful model of Nelson's funeral carriage under a glass dome; gilt bronze fire dogs in the form of Baroque angels; and a quantity of handsome chairs, mostly eighteenth – or early nineteenth-century. There are also seals and, for example, Lord Mottistone's drawing of his new pulpit, dated 1960, given by the Friends of St Paul's to celebrate the 250th anniversary of the completion of the cathedral in 1710. Among the rare books on display is *Lux Ignea* by the Dean of St Paul's, Dr William Sancroft, the text of a sermon preached before King Charles II on 10 October 1666 at a special service following the Great Fire of London.

Chapter Five

THE FURNISHINGS
AND WORKS OF ART

THE DESCRIPTION of the *Furnishings and Works of Art* follows the same order as the *Architectural Walk round the Interior* so that they can be, if desired, used in conjunction with one another or separately. It is recommended that the visitor with less time to spend starts at the north-west entrance and moves round the building clockwise—north nave aisle, dome, north transept, north choir aisle, American Chapel, south choir aisle, south transept, and south nave aisle. This route will provide an opportunity to see most of what is normally accessible, particularly if the crypt (which is entered from the eastern aisle of the south transept) is included as well.

NAVE AISLES AND WESTERN
CHAPELS

Chapel of All Souls

Also known as the Kitchener Memorial Chapel, this is entered from the north-west vestibule but is not normally open except on request. Although not originally planned to serve as a chapel, being the base of the north-west tower, it is of considerable importance artistically as a complete ensemble of the 1920s, planned and executed by a group of architects and sculptors who were all influential members of the Art Workers' Guild, still a potent influence in English artistic life. The architects were Detmar Blow and Sir Mervyn Macartney (the latter then being Surveyor to the Fabric of St Paul's) and the sculptors were Sir George Frampton and Sir William Reid Dick. The chapel is described more fully in the *Tour of the Monuments* (see p. 153).

The Morning Chapel (known as St Dunstan's Chapel since 1905)

Originally requested in order to provide a chapel where the early morning office could be said by the clergy and a small congregation, it was brought into use for this purpose on 1 February 1699. It is normally inaccessible, but two of its most enjoyable attributes—the oak and wrought-iron screens—can be appreciated satisfactorily from the north aisle. The oak screen was the work of the English master-carver Jonathan Maine, and it is balanced by his screen to the Chapel of St Michael and St George on the south. It stands on a low stone base, and consists of a central triumphal arch on coupled columns, and side elements in which Composite columns support an entablature and the spaces between the columns are given free-standing panels low down. The arch is a magnificent climax to the screen, supporting a shield on either side (that to the aisle with the arms of the Dean and Chapter) with three winged cherubs and superb swags of drapery. On either side are pairs of urns with flames issuing forth, symbols of eternity. The gates are topped by scrolls, and the motif used for the frieze is carried round the chapel itself in stone. The chapel is panelled up to the level of the frieze, and the 'aprons' of carved drapery, with tassels and fringes, on the north wall are a delightful touch. Originally the chapel had no altar, and probably only the seating placed round the perimeter. In the nineteenth century the floor level of the eastern apse was raised by three steps and the sanctuary thus created was given a floor of inlaid marble. There is a fine nineteenth-century altar frontal, commemorating St Dunstan (Bishop of London in 959, Archbishop of Canterbury in 960 until his death in 988, and by tradition a painter, musician and metalworker). The altar cross, of painted wood, is an example of the English 'Arts and Crafts' movement, *c*. 1900; and the candlesticks are in a sumptuous Neo-Classical manner, and bear the arms of the Dean and Chapter.

Both apses have been given mosaics. In the eastern apse mosaic decoration fills all five of the moulded panels, the large central one showing Christ displaying His wounds, between the Blessed Virgin and St John the Baptist. The semi-dome, the mouldings, and the frieze have all been gilded or coloured so that the whole forms a convincing decorative scheme. By contrast, in the western apse the central panel alone has a mosaic picture and this shows the *Visit of the Three Marys to the Empty Tomb*. It is by Salviati, and of some historical interest as a memorial to Archdeacon William Hale (d. 1870), who was a notable ecclesiastical reformer and residentiary canon of the cathedral from 1840 until his death.

In the sanctuary there is a framed mosaic panel showing the head of St Paul and, balancing it on the opposite side, a memorial somewhat in the style of Wren to John Howell (d. 1877) which includes, however, a head of Christ crowned with thorns in the manner of the worst religious art of the 1870s. Below the latter is a white marble credence table supported on scrolled brackets, in the style of Wren but probably nineteenth-century. On leaving the chapel particular notice should be given to the splendidly restrained wrought-iron railings, with arrow's head points, provided by Thomas Robinson in 1698–9.

Chapel of St Michael and St George (originally the Consistory Court)

From 1878 to 1894 the Wellington monument was here. Then, for some years, the Chapel was used as a Baptistery. In 1901, following a suggestion made by Archdeacon Sinclair, the Chapel was offered to the Order of the Knights of St Michael and St George as a spiritual home. The Order was founded in 1818. Its members are knighted for distinguished service in overseas territories and foreign affairs and, for example, the present Chancellor of the Order is Lord Carrington, formerly Foreign Secretary and now Secretary General of NATO.

The transformation of the Chapel between 1901 and 1906 was the responsibility of the then Surveyor to the Fabric, Somers Clarke (1841–1926), who later retired to Egypt for the sake of his health, and practised as an architect there. This chapel is, therefore, the most conspicuous evidence of his Surveyorship, and a very rich and remarkable ensemble it is. The dedication of the chapel took place on 12 June 1906. The vault was enriched by the shields of arms of King Edward VII, the Prince of Wales, and the then Chancellor of the Order, Sir Robert Herbert.

The wooden furnishings consist of the reredos in the eastern apse, a throne for the bishop who is Prelate of the Order, the

Detail of the reredos in the Chapel of St Michael and St George (1901–6).

stalls facing inwards for the knights of the Order, and in the western apse a throne for the Sovereign with flanking seats and stalls.

The reredos is a fine composition in the spirit of Wren, with superbly carved figures on the broken pediment and a figure of St George with his sword in one hand and his helmet in the other. In the central niche of the reredos is a much smaller figure, of 1970, by Edwin Russell of a youthful St Michael trampling the devil and his angels underfoot. It is an unusual conception of St Michael, accompanied by five angels who all look rather more like cathedral choristers. On the left of the sanctuary the Prelate's throne incorporates some original seventeenth-century woodwork, and two delightful small figures of bishops with copes, mitres, and crosiers. The royal throne also incorporates Grinling Gibbons carving, and the stalls in the western apse and on the south side all have carved limewood drops which look as though they are from Grinling Gibbons' workshop too. In the stalls are the enamelled heraldic badges of the knights, a fascinating collection; and in the floor are set metal ledgers, also heraldic, of great beauty.

As with the Chapel of St Dunstan opposite, the screen by Jonathan Maine and the iron railings by Thomas Robinson were provided as part of the original fitting out of the western end of the cathedral in the late seventeenth century.

THE DOME AND TRANSEPTS

North Transept

In the western aisle is a terracotta sculpture by Josephina de Vasconcellos of the *Virgin and Child* given in 1957. It is a work of considerable tenderness, and deserves a less half-hearted setting.

In the north-west bay is the font carved by Francis Bird, provided in 1727 at a cost of £350. It is a splendid and richly sculptural object in yellowish blue-veined Carrara marble from Italy, in shape somewhat like a gigantic salt cellar. It is oval, and consists of a base, the bowl itself, and a tiered cover, all of which are made still more magnificent by deep gadrooning. It has occupied several sites in the cathedral since its

OPPOSITE: Virgin and Child (c. 1957), terracotta sculpture by Josephina de Vasconcellos.

Francis Bird's font (1727), which is rather like a gigantic salt cellar.

installation, and its present setting within an enclosure of wooden rails and glazed panels is not perhaps the happiest of them.

The northern part of the north transept is furnished as a chapel in which the Blessed Sacrament is reserved. The sanctuary area contains three fine carved chairs of the Charles II period, a delightful early nineteenth-century chamber organ by R Rycroft of London, an altar of unusual design by John Skelton (1973) in which a central motif based on the Dean and Chapter's arms is flanked by oval columns of engraved glass, fine silver candlesticks, and an altar painting of the *Holy Family and a donor figure*, which is Italian, sixteenth-century. Also deserving of notice and praise is the door to the aumbry carved by the present-day master-carver of the cathedral, Tony Webb, showing the pelican in its piety, an emblem of Christ's self-giving in the Eucharist and on the Cross. The regimental colours are those of the Middlesex Regiment.

The Dome

Here are three items of particular interest, conveniently placed close together. One is the gilt metal eagle lectern (provided in 1720 and made by Jacob Sutton at a cost of £241). There were ample medieval precedents for lecterns whose book-rest was in

LEFT: Tony Webb's aumbry door in the Middlesex Chapel, where the Blessed Sacrament is reserved.
RIGHT: The eagle lectern by Jacob Sutton (1720).

the form of an eagle, and an important consideration for Anglican clergy in the late seventeenth and early eighteenth centuries was to emphasize the continuity with the pre-Reformation Church in England. The eagle is naturalistic, its head raised as though to soar but its claws planted firmly on the support. At the foot of the lectern its base is supported by four beautifully modelled lions.

On the south side of the entrance to the choir is the pulpit, a vigorous essay in the style of Wren—informed, undoubtedly, by a study of those which survive in the City churches by Wren—designed by Lord Mottistone in 1960, and brought into use in 1964. As with the original furnishings in the choir it is a combination of oak and lime, and the limewood carvings on the waist of the pulpit and on the canopy are beautifully done. The canopy carries an openwork cupola with an elegantly designed urn as its finial, and round the cupola winged cherubs and urns hold up heavy swags of flowers. The two *putti* bear aloft the collar and badge of the Order of St Michael and St George. The panel below the canopy supports, as is traditional, a Crucifixion and this is a fine work of modern sculpture by Edwin Russell.

Between the pulpit and the lectern is a low ironwork screen, now serving as the choir screen but originally provided as the Communion rail, by Jean Tijou, in the time of Wren. Its principal motifs are scrolls and acanthus leaves and a series of small heads set in profile.

The mosaic decoration in the area of the dome is important aesthetically both in preparing the eye for the greater splendour of the decoration in the choir and also in complementing in the lower zone the paintings by Sir James Thornhill in the dome itself. The work of three significant nineteenth-century artists is represented here—Alfred George Stevens, George Frederick Watts, and William Blake Richmond—together with that of a lesser-known figure, W E Britten.

Better known as a sculptor, and in particular as the sculptor of the Wellington monument in St Paul's Cathedral, in the early 1860s in the time of Dean Milman, Alfred Stevens produced designs and a large model for the redecoration of the dome with mosaic and sculpture. It proved too controversial to tackle the dome itself, and so a start was made with the enrichment of the spandrels beneath. The intention was to have mosaics of the four Evangelists (Matthew, Mark, Luke and John) and the four major prophets (Isaiah, Jeremiah, Ezekiel and Daniel). Work on Isaiah, following Alfred Stevens's cartoon, was carried out by the firm of Salviati of Venice and was finished in July 1864. The next mosaic, depicting St Matthew, was by G F Watts. Meanwhile, in May 1863, a Decoration Committee had been established by the Dean and Chapter and an appeal for funds had been launched in which the proposal for an all-embracing scheme of decoration was described. Part of this scheme was to fill the principal windows with stained glass, and part was for 'filling the spandrels of the dome and vaults, and other suitable compartments, and ultimately the dome itself, with paintings in mosaic, and for spandrels nearer the eye, in the use of a species of mosaic, formed by inlaid marbles, similar to the work of Beccafumi in Siena Cathedral; and generally in gilding and incrusting, with coloured marbles, parts of the architecture to complete the decorative framework.' The cost of filling the eight spandrels of the dome with mosaic was

OPPOSITE: *Three stages of decoration in the dome area: in the bottom left-hand corner is G F Watts's mosaic of St Luke (1860s) in one of the spandrels; on the surface of the inner dome is the cycle of paintings of scenes from the life of St Paul by Sir James Thornhill (completed 1720); and in the semi-dome at the top of the picture is a mosaic of the 1890s by Sir William Blake Richmond.*

given as being about £650 each; and, in addition, the 'four semicupolas where the vaulting of the aisle intersects the dome would admit of grand subjects, such as the Nativity and Baptism of Our Lord, etc, at a cost of about £1,000 each. The upper semidome and the adjoining great arches of the dome might be finished for about £300 each.'

After this brave start, comparatively little money came in and comparatively little was done until 1872. Then, following a service of thanksgiving for the recovery of the Prince of Wales from typhoid, money became available in sufficiently large quantities for a new start to be made and the talented architect William Burges was appointed jointly with the Surveyor to the Fabric, F C Penrose, to produce a scheme. Still more controversy was aroused by Burges's proposals, the full story of which can be read in J Mordaunt Crook's book *William Burges and the High Victorian Dream* (1981); and so a further moratorium followed until 1878, when the Dean and Chapter acquired the model for the dome mosaic by Alfred Stevens, who by this time had died. Lord Leighton and Sir Edward Poynter, two of the best-known painters of the day, were also asked to prepare cartoons for different aspects of the scheme; but these plans, once again, came to nothing. In the *Autobiography* of Dean Robert Gregory (d. 1911) the following passage occurs: 'About two things to be done there was perfect unanimity of opinion. The one was that the remaining spandrels in the dome should be filled with mosaics. Designs for them had been generously given by Mr. Stevens and Mr. Watts. These were duly enlarged, and the work was entrusted to Messrs. Salviati of Venice, who had executed the two that were already in position.' He omits to mention that the supervision of this work was in the hands of W E Britten, who was permitted to design St Mark and St Luke himself.

In 1891 the architects Bodley and Garner, who were responsible for the design of an immense reredos behind the high altar, suggested to the Dean and Chapter the involvement of yet another artist for the completion of a scheme of mosaics, William Blake Richmond; and by him are the mosaics in the semidomes over the diagonal corners of the dome, and in the galleries above them. By him also is the whole scheme of mosaic decoration in the choir and its aisles, which will be described later.

Parentalia speaks laconically of the painted decoration of the dome above: 'The Inside of the whole Cupola is painted, and richly decorated, by an eminent English artist, Sir James Thornhill, containing, in eight Compartments, the Histories of St. Paul. In the Crown of the Vault, as in the Pantheon, is a circular Opening, by which not only the Lantern transmits Light, but the Inside Ornaments of the painted and gilded Cone, display a new and agreeable Scene.' A footnote explains that 'The Judgment of the Surveyor was originally, instead of painting in the Manner it is now perform'd, to have beautified the Inside of the Cupola with the more durable Ornament of Mosaick-work, as is nobly executed in the Cupola of St. Peter's in Rome, which strikes the Eye of the Beholder with a most magnificent and splendid Appearance'; but, tactfully, no mention is made of the controversy over the designs. Five artists submitted proposals: Wren was not particularly enthusiastic about any of them but, on the whole, thought that those by the Italian artist, Antonio Pellegrini, were the best; whereupon the Dean and Chapter chose Thornhill's. The matter was referred to the Archbishop of Canterbury for arbitration, and he decided that the artist should be both Protestant and an Englishman, and so Thornhill received the commission.

The paintings were carried out in oil technique on plaster, and are in monochrome (that is, only one colour is deployed over a stone-coloured background); by lavish use of gold an impression of great richness is achieved. The most obvious feature of the design is the way in which the eight 'Histories of St Paul' are contained within a framework of illusionistic architecture in the form of eight great arches, whose pillars and interstices are painted with a splendid scheme of illusionistic sculpture. The scenes from the life of St Paul represent his conversion, the punishment of Elymas the sorcerer, the cure of the cripple at Lystra, the conversion of the jailer, St Paul preaching at Athens, the Ephesians burning books, St Paul before Agrippa, and the shipwreck at Malta. The inner circle is painted with coffering of diminishing sizes, and more painted coffering can be seen on the crown of the brick cone above.

The work was completed by 1720, and Thornhill was paid a total of £6,575. He presented King George I with an engraved set of designs, and received a knighthood. Thornhill was undoubtedly one of the outstanding English decorative painters of the Baroque era and this, his most ambitious scheme, can be enjoyed in its own right even though some slight hesitation may remain as to whether it truly and effectively complements Wren's massively dignified architecture.

In the zone below the painted dome are eight large-scale figures in stone of what Dean Gregory called 'the four eastern and four western most illustrious doctors of the Church': the eastern doctors are Athanasius, Basil, Gregory of Nazianzus, and Chrysostom, and the western doctors are Ambrose, Augustine, Jerome and Gregory. C E Kempe designed them, and they were carried out in 1892–4 by the carver Frederick Winnington, who worked for the firm of Farmer and Brindley.

Although the screens and gates into the choir aisles belong physically to the eastern arm of the building they belong visually to the area of the dome, from where they are best seen. They are part of that astonishing complement of decorative metalwork provided for Wren by Jean Tijou which, together with Grinling Gibbons's woodwork, make the furnishings of the choir as exciting an ensemble artistically speaking as can be found in any great church in Europe of the same date. These screens are very architectural in concept, with Corinthian columns framing the central gates, and a cornice above—transmuted airily into metal from the more usual stone or wood—and above them are tripartite over-throws of delicate ornament. They are painted black, not gilded like those flanking the sanctuary, and are a little later in date by about a dozen years. Tijou himself designed all the metalwork he supplied to the cathedral, but he was required to do so in close consultation with Wren; the joiners had to supply him with large boards on which the pattern could be drawn out in detail, for discussion with Wren and for his approval.

The South Transept

The only significant furnishing here is the internal porch with a gallery over it which, as explained elsewhere, was made out of portions of the screen or pulpitum which Wren had provided to stand across the west end of the choir and to support the organ. The two marble columns appear to have belonged to that screen. Other portions of the screen were worked into a similar porch-gallery for the north transept, but this was destroyed in the Second World War. On this surviving porch the carving of the capitals of the wooden columns, and the panels of the frieze between the capitals, is of quite exceptional quality and beauty. It is, of course, from the workshop of Grinling Gibbons. The balustrade was added in 1965, and the glazed inner doors in 1968.

LEFT: *One of the scenes from the 'Histories of St Paul' by Sir James Thornhill (completed in 1720), framed in painted illusionistic architecture.*
RIGHT: *Grinling Gibbons's choir stalls and the organ all in their original positions before being moved in the 1860s; from the completion of the building until that time the organ stood on a screen towards the west end of the choir.*

THE CHOIR, AISLES AND EASTERN CHAPELS

The visitor normally enters the eastern arm of the building through the gate into the north choir aisle, and this description will follow the same clockwise direction round the eastern apse and back down the south aisle. First, however, it seems desirable to describe the major furnishings and decoration of the choir itself (access to which is by means of joining one of the special tours). A good general view may be had by standing at the entrance to the choir on the eastern side of the dome: the overwhelming impression is of glorious colour, gilding, and light in the upper zone where the walls above the entablature of the arcade and the vault are encrusted with mosaics, and in the lower zone it is the woodwork of Grinling

Gibbons's choir stalls which predominates. Uniting the two zones are the pair of organ cases at the west end, and the baldacchino over the high altar at the east.

Before describing the furnishings as we now see them it is necessary to recapture something of the original arrangement, as shown in the illustration. This shows that the organ was on a screen towards the west end of the choir. When this screen was removed in 1860 the organ was at first placed on the north side of the choir. (Its removal from this position later on in the nineteenth century is the second of the two matters over which Dean Gregory wrote in his *Autobiography* that there was 'perfect unanimity of opinion': 'The other alteration was the removal of the organ from under one of the arches on the north side of the choir, whither it had been placed a few years previously, having stood before that time on the screen at the west end of the choir. It was now placed against the north and south walls at the west end of the choir.') The stalls originally came a little further west, into the middle of the west bay of the choir, and were then 'returned' (that is, the stalls for the dignitaries of the cathedral were placed with their backs against the screen, facing east, instead of being as at present facing inwards behind the choir stalls and below the organ cases on either side). This arrangement, which survives in various forms in those cathedrals where there is still a solid screen or pulpitum (e.g. York, Lincoln, Norwich, Rochester, Canterbury, Wells and Exeter), gave the choir a true sense of enclosure as the place where the daily round of services, the *opus Dei*, was celebrated, whereas the nave, with its larger capacity, was for a more public use. The nineteenth-century enthusiasm for removing solid screens (as at Durham and Salisbury) arose from a quite different ecclesiological viewpoint from that obtaining in the Middle Ages or in the time of Wren: visually it was thought desirable to be able to experience the building without significant interruption from west to east, and liturgically the use of the cathedral was conceived as being like that of a parish church, only on the grandest possible scale, with the 'action' by clergy and choir going on at the east end clearly visible to the somewhat passive congregation in the nave. Present-day ecclesiology rather tends to the earlier view, with a distinction being made between the services in the choir attended by the cathedral community—whose very *raison d'être* is the daily offering of worship to the highest possible standards, liturgically and musically speaking—and such visitors or pilgrims who happen to be there, on the one hand; and, on the other, those occasions when the cathedral is in use by what might be called its 'extended family', whether diocesan or national or associated with some special organization or event, when the nave comes into its own and, in many cathedrals, where the nave has its own permanent altar and sanctuary.

The altar in Wren's original arrangement was in the eastern apse, where the altar of the American Chapel is today. The wrought-iron Communion rail which at present closes off the choir at its western end was the rail provided by Jean Tijou for the high altar, and was already the second Communion rail provided.

The Mosaic Decoration

The intention in Wren's mind, as has been mentioned elsewhere (p. 99), seems to have been to decorate the entire interior with mosaic and gilding. Had he carried out his intentions his idiom would have been that of the Baroque, not—as we have it now—the vocabulary of the Byzantine world as interpreted by late nineteenth-century English eyes. The story of how St Paul's came to have the strong scheme of mosaic decoration in the choir and choir aisles is superbly well told in J Mordaunt Crook's book *William Burges and the High Victorian Dream*. Here it must suffice to say that the first serious attempt, in which a scheme was prepared by William Burges (whose polychromatic interiors for the third Marquess of Bute can still be seen at Castle Coch, Cardiff Castle and the church of St Mary, Studley Royal, in West Yorkshire), failed: it aroused much articulate controversy and would have been extremely expensive, and there was perhaps insufficient will power to push it through in the face of well-organized opposition. Burges's scheme envisaged refacing the whole of the interior of the cathedral with a veneer of richly polished marbles, interspersed with mosaics, and with the carved ornament of the cathedral enriched with gilding: white was to have predominated near the ground but, as the eye rose, it would encounter blacks, reds, blues, greens and gold; and as the eye moved not only upwards but also eastwards so, also, would the splendour and richness have been increased. Having launched an appeal in the summer of 1870, the Dean and Chapter finally conceded the weight of opinion against the scheme in November 1874, and Burges was paid for the substantial amount of preparatory work which he had done.

LEFT: The mosaic decoration in the apse, Christ the King flanked by cherubim and seraphim, juxtaposed with the interior of the dome of the baldacchino.
RIGHT: Detail of one of the seraphim flanking Christ the King, the centrepiece of Sir William Richmond's mosaic decoration of the 1890s in a style which might be called Byzantine Art Nouveau.

In the 1880s there was a scheme for covering over Thornhill's paintings in the dome with a series of paintings illustrating the Book of Revelation. Designs were actually prepared, and suspended over Thornhill's paintings in 1883 to assess their impact; but in due course the project was dropped.

In April 1883 the Chapter invited G F Bodley to prepare designs for a new high altar and an appropriate setting for it; and the result was an impressive design for a lofty reredos of many different marbles, reaching to clerestory level and carried out between August 1886 and January 1888. In 1891 a new high altar was given, to complete the ensemble, and in the space behind the reredos the Jesus Chapel (now the American Chapel) was formed. The reredos undoubtedly provided a magnificent and climactic setting for the high altar though, at the same time, it obscured the apse which Wren had intended as the architectural and visual climax to the building.

Soon after the installation of Dean Gregory in February

1891 the suggestion was made to him that Sir William Blake Richmond (as he later became) should be employed to provide designs for mosaic decoration of the eastern arm of the building. This suggestion was approved of by the Decoration Committee, and arrangements for the implementation of the scheme were almost immediately put in hand. By November 1892 the easternmost saucer dome of the choir was completed, and approved of; and the work carried out steadily, amidst tremendous public interest and enthusiasm, until in March 1896 the vault of the choir was finished and the remainder of the work in the eastern arm a year later. The series of mosaics representing prophets and evangelists in the spandrels of the dome, which had been begun in the early 1860s, was completed between 1892 and 1894; and mosaics were inserted in the quarter domes under the Whispering Gallery between 1898 and 1901, paid for by various City companies. The aisles of the choir were not completed until August 1907.

The principal themes of the decoration of the choir vault are taken from the canticle known as the *Benedicite* ('O all ye works of the Lord, praise ye the Lord'). The subject of the decoration of the three saucer domes is announced by the Latin texts (from west to east):

OMNES BESTIAE ET PECORA

(O ALL YE BEASTS AND CATTLE)

OMNES QUAE MOVENTUR IN AQUIS

(O YE WHALES, AND ALL THAT MOVE IN THE WATERS)

OMNES VOLUCRES COELI

(O ALL YE FOWLS OF THE AIR)

In the first saucer dome from the west various beasts of the field are seen disporting themselves in a landscape of gently rounded hills, with stylized palm trees set at regular intervals. The whole scene is surrounded by a black text on a gold ground, supported in the spandrels by four magnificent seraphim (as in the other two bays). In the middle saucer dome are whales, dolphins, and various different kinds of fish with great spouts of water from the mouths of the whales. And in the easternmost saucer dome are the feathered fowls of the air, including a number of water-loving birds, in a paradisical landscape of water, trees and hills beneath a golden sky.

There are also mosaics in the spandrels of the arcade, most effectively using the spaces available, and showing (on the north side, west to east) the Creation, the Annunciation, and two seraphim and (on the south side) the Expulsion of Adam and Eve, the Temptation of Adam and Eve, and two more seraphim with the admonition 'Watch and Pray'.

There are further mosaics in the clerestory zone, six pairs of scenes either side of the windows; and on either side of the high sanctuary, but difficult to see because of the later baldacchino, are two further mosaic panels.

The climax of the whole scheme is the figure of Christ the King, seated in majesty on a rainbow with both his hands raised in blessing, in the centre panel of the apse vault with cherubim and seraphim clad in superb vestments, and with gilded wings, in the side panels.

The Organ

The organ was commissioned in 1694 from Bernard Schmidt (known, frequently, as 'Father Smith') and the carving of the casework was carried out in Grinling Gibbons's workshop. Originally it stood on a solid screen or pulpitum at the west end of the choir, and was only moved from this position (and then to a temporary position on the north side of the choir) in 1860. In 1872 the case was divided, and the two halves placed where we see them now. The case on the south side was the one originally facing westwards into the dome, but its subsidiary chair case is that which was formerly facing into the choir; the case on the north side was originally the eastward-facing case, but its subsidiary chair case is a nineteenth-century facsimile, to balance visually that placed on the south. The creation of this facsimile case was, by any standards, a remarkable achievement as it fits most convincingly into the surrounding panoply of original seventeenth-century woodwork. The splendour of the seventeenth-century carvings, which include numerous large-scale figure sculptures, makes this without doubt the most sculptural and spectacular of all English organ cases surviving from the late seventeenth or early eighteenth centuries. All the show pipes are gilded, which complements the magnificently rich effect of the carving.

OPPOSITE: A detail of Grinling Gibbons's carving on the organ case, combining figure sculpture with draperies, acanthus and wreaths of flowers.

The Choir Stalls

The choir stalls carry on this theme of richness in their carving. First, however, their actual disposition must be described. On the north side, counting from the east, are first six pairs of stalls for prebendaries, priests who work in the diocese of London but are members of the Greater Chapter of the cathedral: every prebendary has to recite daily a particular psalm, and over his stall the first words of his psalm are picked out in gilt lettering, together with the place-name from which the prebendary takes his title. Behind these stalls are galleries, like boxes in a theatre or opera house, for the families of the prebendaries. Then comes a stall for the Lord Mayor of London. His stall takes the form of a shell-headed niche above which, and enclosed by the pediment of a canopy, is ravishingly delicate carved ornament of flowers and foliage; above the pediment is a panel carved with two *putti* carrying emblems of the Lord Mayor's high office, the sword symbolizing justice (the Lord Mayor is the chief magistrate of the City of London) and the mace symbolizing authority and good government.

Then follow seven more pairs of stalls but here, in six bays out of seven, the 'opera boxes' are replaced by carved and pierced panels concealing rooms behind. Beneath the organ cases on the north and south sides are the stalls for the principal dignitaries of the cathedral, the dean and the canons who form the Residentiary Chapter, who are the legal owners of St Paul's Cathedral and all that belongs to it.

Over both sides of the stalls project deep canopies, supported on brackets which take the form alternatively of *putti* and openwork scrolls. There are thirteen such *putti* on either side, and each one is a masterpiece of the carver's art. The canopy fronts are carved with a dynamically flowing pattern of boldly projecting scrolls, and between each pair of scrolls is a winged cherub's head adorned with ribbons. Between the brackets which support the canopy are swags of flowers and foliage.

The disposition on the south side is similar to the north, but with some differences. The open galleries or 'opera boxes', for example, are here continued on both sides of the central canopied stall, which is for the use of the Bishop of London when he is sitting 'in choir'. Within the pedimented canopy of his stall is an exceptionally beautiful area of applied carving, showing the pelican in its piety (an emblem of Christ's self-giving, an example which a bishop must strive to emulate); and above it is an eagle and a serpent. The upper part of the canopy has two *putti* supporting a mitre, symbol of the bishop's office and authority. Here, as throughout the stalls, the applied carving is of limewood whereas the stalls themselves are of oak.

The other chief difference on the south side is that the range of stalls terminates at the east end in the bishop's throne, for use when he attends in state on great occasions. This is one of the most inventive pieces of design in the whole cathedral, the canopy being supported on two columns richly carved with trails of foliage and flowers, and its front taking the form of a segmental scroll adorned with palm fronds. The entablature supports an attic stage with a full range of applied ornament, including winged cherubs' heads and drops of flowers and foliage; and above that are two further openwork tiers with more winged cherubs' heads and garlands trailing diagonally and, finally, on top is the episcopal mitre.

Within the bishop's throne is a chair of quite exceptional quality. A high-backed chair, with arms which curve vigorously outwards, its front legs are a study in graceful adornment; the swept-up back incorporates the arms of the Dean and Chapter with those of Henry Compton, Bishop of London during the building of the cathedral. It is extremely moving to think of him using that chair when the choir of the new cathedral was inaugurated at a service in December 1697.

Baldacchino and High Altar

From this point the baldacchino and high altar can be studied to good advantage, while remembering that they were also intended to be seen from further away. They were designed by Stephen Dykes Bower and W Godfrey Allen, and completed in 1958.

The altar is an exceptionally long one, its length dictated by the enormous scale of the cathedral itself; it is of white marble, skilfully designed in the vocabulary of Wren, and the front panels are carved with emblems of the Eucharist (grapes and ears of wheat representing the wine and bread used in the celebration of the Eucharist). On the altar stand a lofty cross and a pair of candlesticks, Classical-Baroque in style, made of gilt metal, and also designed by that twentieth-century master, Stephen Dykes Bower. They were the generous gift of the Worshipful Company of Goldsmiths.

The baldacchino is a canopy of honour over the high altar, and its source—both in the mind of Wren, as evidenced in

Parentalia, and in the minds of Stephen Dykes Bower and W
Godfrey Allen as exemplified by the design—was Bernini's
canopy over the high altar in St Peter's in Rome. Its associa-
tions are, therefore, of the highest; and both in its aspirations
and in its forms it provides us with a suitably exalted climax to
the whole building at the very point where that climax,
visually and emotionally, needs to be: over the high altar. The
four corners are supported by a trio of columns: two are fluted,
one square and one round, and the third column in the most
prominent position is in the same form as the twisted columns
of Bernini's canopy in Rome. Bernini's columns were, in their
turn, an evocation of the columns of the temple of Solomon in
Jerusalem. These columns stand on bases of white marble
(otherwise the baldacchino is of wood, richly gilded in many
of its parts), and support a massive entablature. To the north
and south are triangular pediments, and to the west and east are
broken segmental pediments of heroic proportions. From these
broken pediments are suspended tassels of painted and gilded
wood, taking up the by-now-familiar theme of winged
cherubs' heads.

Above and within the framework established by the pedimented sides rises an elliptical dome, supported on a tall attic
stage pierced with oval openings which are themselves richly
ornamented. Four gilded urns, with flames issuing forth, stand
round the attic stage. On the gilded cupola of the dome stands
a figure of the risen Christ, his right hand extended in
benediction; while, to left and right, stand angels in postures of
adoration.

The achievement of this baldacchino cannot be too highly
stressed. Throughout the nineteenth century much energy had
been expended, by clergy and architects, in devising a fitting
climax to St Paul's; yet none was imagined or realized as
successfully as this. In addition, so many twentieth-century
attempts to use a historical style have been unsatisfactory, even
spectacularly so in some cases. Yet this one succeeds, and it is
reasonable to wonder why. It can surely only be because those
responsible for it, thoroughly versed as they were in the
language of Baroque and Classical architecture and deeply
imbued with the spirit of Wren's building, believed in what
they were doing and brought to it total conviction. It is as
simple as that.

Placed near the high altar, on either side, are two superb
bronze candlesticks with rich Renaissance ornament. These are

One of the gate-screens flanking the high sanctuary, in which Tijou's original metalwork of the 1690s is set within a framework by Bodley and Garner of 1890.

casts taken from a pair in the church of St Bavon at Ghent, in Belgium; the originals are ascribed to Benedetto da Rovez-zano, and are thought to have been made to accompany Cardinal Wolsey's sarcophagus, now to be found in the crypt of St Paul's as the sarcophagus of Admiral Viscount Nelson (see p. 144).

Facing into both the choir and aisles are two sets of gate-screens on either side. The larger sets are placed in the easternmost of the three principal arches of the main arcade, and are sumptuously gilded. They include elements which were originally below the organ screen, when it was placed at the west end of the choir, and they have been expanded to fit their situation here. The original parts include, on the south side, seated figures of St Paul and St Peter; and, on the north side, four ravishingly beautiful roundels of the four Evangelists in the act of writing their Gospels and accompanied by their attributes (a man for St Matthew, a lion for St Mark, an ox for St Luke, and an eagle for St John). The pilasters of the Composite order, incorporating figures of the twelve Apostles in tiny Renaissance-style aedicules, and the cornices and candlesticks are all part of the late nineteenth-century remodelling; and are extremely well done. The date 1890 appears on both sides.

The smaller sets of gate-screens are placed in the short bays just west of the apse, and they appear to be entirely original to the time of Tijou and Wren. They have fine gilded scrollwork done with all Tijou's customary panache, and elaborate overthrows on which candles in their holders rise and fall.

Stained Glass

The stained glass in the six windows of the apse is all by Brian Thomas, *c.* 1960. The windows are in two tiers, and the subject matter of the three lower ones consists of Scenes from the Life of Christ: the central window depicts the Crucifixion; that on the left the Adoration of the Three Kings, Washing the Disciples' Feet, and Driving the Money Changers from the Temple; and that on the right the Placing of Jesus in the Sepulchre, the Empty Tomb, and the Resurrection. The artist has described how the commission for the three lower windows came about as a result of his membership of the Art Workers' Guild, of which the Surveyor to the Fabric (W Godfrey Allen) was then the Master. 'The windows were duly installed, and the Dean saw me at the morning service. He asked me if I would design the smaller windows as well. But he said that no-one could suggest a suitable subject. I therefore asked the intelligent curate of my local church, and without hesitation he suggested the I AM texts of St John's Gospel. I relayed this suggestion to the Dean who said "Yes, of course!" ' The predominant tones are blues and golds, and they complement the mosaic-work and the baldacchino admirably. The iconography is not so important, perhaps, as the general effect when seen from a distance—which gives colour and richness at the extreme east end of the building. The Crucifixion seems to have been inspired by the relief sculpture by John Singer Sargent in the crypt, which is one of the lesser-known masterpieces of St Paul's (see pp. 137, 138).

The Choir Aisles

In the choir aisles the programme of mosaic decoration by Richmond is continued. On the north side this begins with an image of Christ the Reaper, sitting and holding sheaves of corn; and the whole of the central panel of that western bay is

Detail of Brian Thomas's Crucifixion in the central east window (c. 1960).

decorated with trails of vine and grapes and with anthemion ornament. The next bay shows seraphim holding anchors against a backdrop of ships in full sail on a sea of stylized waves. The following bay shows warrior seraphim holding shields, swords and bugles against a backdrop of paradisical flowers. The next shows seraphim alternating with sheaves of corn and holding various attributes, for example, a sickle and a basket. Finally the east bay shows Apollo playing his lyre (a symbol of creativity), surrounded by winged lions and horses and Renaissance-style ornament.

One of the greatest visual pleasures of the two choir aisles is the backs of the choir stalls, which fill two bays on either side. Made, like the choir stalls themselves, in the workshop of Grinling Gibbons between 1695 and 1697, each bay forms an elegant composition: a central doorway is framed by pairs of columns which support an entablature with a balustrade on top formed of wonderfully carved balusters, and on either side are subsidiary doorways. Within and above the door in every bay are pierced panels—twenty-four in all—with ironwork grilles by Jean Tijou, each in its way a paradigm of design and craftsmanship. The upper grilles are framed by garlands of flowers by Grinling Gibbons.

In the floor of the aisles, as elsewhere in the cathedral, are magnificent brass grilles, through which can be glimpsed the crypt below. These were installed in 1881, to replace an earlier set in cast-iron installed in 1858, their purpose being to allow warm air from a heating system below to rise and circulate round the cathedral as a whole. Archdeacon William Hale, who became a canon of the cathedral in 1840, had previously caused a kind of wagon to be drawn about the floor of the cathedral, filled with hot coals, so great was his determination to find a satisfactory method of heating the building. Canon Sydney Smith, a fellow member of the Chapter and a renowned letter-writer, told him that 'the only real way of doing it is to warm the County of Middlesex'. The grilles became redundant in 1909, when a system of hot-water heating was installed.

In the first two bays of the north choir aisle are the music library and a small vestry, each enclosed by panelling. That in the middle bay, with a triangular pediment, is a memorial to those former St Paul's choristers who died in the First World War; it was designed by Sir Mervyn Macartney. It is a strikingly handsome piece of its date (c. 1925), and shows how even minor furnishings in a building like St Paul's can be—and ought to be—of a certain distinction; it has good carving, and excellent lettering.

Also in the north choir aisle are preserved two organ consoles, one from the period 1900–25 and the other from the period 1925–76. The latter has a music desk carved in the manner of Grinling Gibbons.

In the third bay the superb gilded screens framing the sanctuary may be enjoyed from the outside. The double gates in the middle, and the side panels, were made by Jean Tijou and stood beneath the organ screen at the west end of the choir. The four roundels with the Evangelists and their symbols are original, and are particularly enjoyable. The gilded pilasters and entablature were added in 1890 under the supervision of

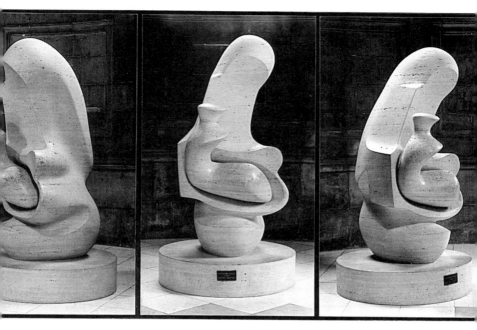

Henry Moore's Mother and Child sculpture (1983) does not yield up its significance from a single viewpoint. These three aspects suggest the ideas of conception, generation within the womb, and infancy and motherhood.

G F Bodley, of Bodley and Garner, at the time when the screens were installed here.

From this position on either side it is possible to look up and see the sumptuous richness of the mosaic panels flanking the clerestory windows (whose ironwork was provided by Tijou's workshop in 1691) and at the gallery level below.

In the north choir aisle at this point is Henry Moore's *Mother and Child* sculpture in Travertine stone, placed here in 1983. The sculptor himself chose this site for it, where it can be enjoyed as a freestanding work. It is a beautiful and tender piece, evoking the pathos as well as the joy of motherhood; the tilt of the mother's head suggests a premonition of suffering and death as well as joy; compassion and sorrow as well as protectiveness and pride.

The east end of the north aisle is the Modern Martyrs Chapel, formed here in 1962. It has an altar in the Classical style made of wood painted to look like marble, with small marble panels inset. Over it is the fine Crucifixion sculpture from the former Bodley and Garner high altar reredos of 1886–8.

The eastern apse behind the high altar and baldacchino is furnished as the American Memorial Chapel, dedicated on 26 November 1958. The floor of black and white marble, the altar with its sun-burst throw-over frontal, the reredos, cross and candlesticks, the curved stalls, the Communion rail, and the casket for the Roll of Honour listing all those members of the American forces who gave their lives in the Second World War were all designed by Stephen Dykes Bower and W Godfrey Allen. It is a superbly successful ensemble, not only in its overall conception but also in its well-executed detail. Of particularly good quality are the eight carved limewood drops on the pilasters of the reredos and stalls, which were all carved by George Haslop. They depict American birds, fruit and flowers and give abundant proof that the highest craft skills are not lacking in the second half of the twentieth century: what *are* generally lacking are sufficient opportunities, without which artists and craftsmen are unable to develop their skills and their confidence.

The east end of the south aisle is furnished as a Lady Chapel, and its focus is the sculpture of the Blessed Virgin Mary and the Child Jesus taken from the same Bodley and Garner reredos as the Crucifixion in the equivalent chapel on the north side.

The Communion table is that made by William Samwell at Wren's direction, as the original high altar and, as such, it is an immensely important piece of late seventeenth-century liturgical furnishing. On it stand an eighteenth-century Rococo cross and candlesticks from southern Germany, the gift of the West German nation in 1958. The Virgin and Child sculpture is framed by late seventeenth-century woodwork, re-used, with two *putti* holding garlands.

The mosaic panel over the Lady Chapel altar shows Our Lady seated above the world, in a posture of sorrow or compassion. The next bay west has mosaic decoration echoing the equivalent one on the north side; the middle saucer dome has seraphim playing musical instruments against a landscape of rounded hills and snow-capped mountains; and the third has seraphim holding scrolls alternating with the walls and gates of the heavenly Jerusalem. The final short bay at the west end of the aisle shows Christ the Good Shepherd, balancing Christ the Reaper on the other side.

At the west end of the nave stand two magnificent bronze candelabra, modelled by the sculptor Henry Pegram, 1898. In the south aisle hangs one of the three versions of W Holman Hunt's painting *The Light of the World*, signed and dated 1851–1900.

THE CRYPT

The East End of the Crypt

This was known anciently as St Faith-under-St-Paul's, and the memory of this name is still maintained. However, on 12 May 1960 the eastern end was rededicated as the Chapel of the Most Excellent Order of the British Empire. As in the case of the American Memorial Chapel and the Chapel of St Michael and St George, the furnishings form a remarkably complete ensemble of their period. They were designed by the then Surveyor to the Fabric, Lord Mottistone, in collaboration with the artist Brian Thomas who was responsible for the stained glass—as in the choir above—and also for the engraved glass on the screens.

The altar has a throw-over frontal of deep red velvet with the badge of the Order in gold and silver thread. The motto is 'For God and Empire'. The Baroque-style chairs and the charming font in silvered wood all form part of this ensemble. The most ambitious aspect of the furnishing, artistically speaking, is the screen which surrounds the sanctuary of the chapel. This is of black-painted wrought iron, in a Baroque style incorporating sixteen panels of engraved glass. On the left side of the entrance are shown King George V and Queen Mary, and on the right side Queen Elizabeth II and HRH Prince Philip; the panels behind the altar show Queen Elizabeth the Queen Mother and the late George VI. The remainder of the panels (each one of which is a delightful work of art) show animals, activities, landscape, buildings and people emblematic of the diverse parts of the formerly far-flung British Empire. The cross and candlesticks on the altar are also of wrought iron, and of commendable delicacy. Lord Mottistone also designed special Communion silver for the chapel, dedicated in October 1963 and usually on display in the cathedral Treasury.

The Central Part of the Crypt

In the north aisle, close to the Nelson sarcophagus, are displayed in a glass case memorabilia of Sir Christopher Wren including a plaster cast of the marble bust by Edward Pierce which is in the Ashmolean Museum, Oxford; his ceremonial measuring rod (with 'Surveyor to the Fabric' painted on it) used, apparently, at the formal opening of St Paul's; his pen-knife and knife-case; his death-mask; and an engraving of the portrait by Sir Godfrey Kneller.

In another case is a seventeenth-century felt cap, which belonged to one of the craftsmen who worked on the building of St Paul's; and some examples of Jean Tijou's ironwork.

At the entrance to the Treasury are three large wooden models, well worth studying: (i) A model of one of the eight piers supporting the dome, showing the whole system from foundation level to the inner brick cone, c. 1920. (ii) A white-painted model showing half of the top of the brick cone, the stone lantern, and the gilded ball and cross (early nineteenth-century). (iii) A block model, contemporary with (i), showing part of the dome area and the system of reinforcement carried out between 1925 and 1930.

Two examples of carving from the workshop of Grinling Gibbons are also shown here, and probably came from the original pulpitum or organ screen taken down in the nineteenth century.

The Treasury

The Treasury, opened in the north transept of the crypt in 1981, is a collection of fine metalwork, vestments, and other treasures from both St Paul's cathedral and also chiefly from churches in the diocese of London. The entrance gates are by an outstanding young artist-blacksmith from Gloucestershire, Alan Evans. The collection of treasures from St Paul's includes the altar silver (cross and candlesticks) and Communion service provided for the Chapel of St Michael and St George. The gilded Communion service was designed and made by William Bainbridge Reynolds (1855–1935), an architect and metalworker whose work is always of exceptional interest. The church of St Cuthbert, Philbeach Gardens, in Kensington was transformed by the ravishingly beautiful metalwork he created for it and, by happy chance, a leather, silver and enamel book cover made by him for St Cuthbert's is also in the Treasury. Also made by him is the enamelled morse, for use in the same

Chapel, which was designed by Princess Marie-Louise of Schleswig-Holstein, a grand-daughter of Queen Victoria. The Communion service for the Chapel of the Most Excellent Order of the British Empire is also on display: this was designed by Lord Mottistone, and therefore forms part of the ensemble of furnishings and works of art designed and co-ordinated by him for that Chapel (1960).

The vestments usually on display include the cope worn by Bishop Mandell Creighton at Queen Victoria's Diamond Jubilee Service in 1897, and another cope worn on the same occasion. Also shown is the 'Jubilee' cope, stole and mitre designed by Beryl Dean and made 1975–7 for Bishop Gerald Ellison to wear during the present Queen's Silver Jubilee service in the cathedral in June 1977. Communion vessels, churchwardens' staves, and other items of historic metalwork are shown in great profusion.

The Great Model

In the central vessel of the nave is displayed the Great Model, one of the largest and most magnificent architectural models in the world. It was made, on the orders of King Charles II and to Wren's instructions, in 1673–4; and a precedent for the construction of such a large-scale model was that made of Antonio da Sangallo's plans for the completion of St Peter's in Rome. The Great Model was made in the Convocation House by the master-joiner William Cleere, and his staff of a dozen men; they constructed a special table and frame for the model, and trestle tables on which the designs were drawn out on boards of grained wood to the correct scale. Richard Cleere carved the capitals and other fine ornament inside and out, and it is said that the youthful Grinling Gibbons carved tiny figures for the skyline, though if so these have disappeared. (The Model underwent a period of neglect in the early nineteenth century, and was lent to the South Kensington Museum in 1857 on condition that it was satisfactorily repaired. In c. 1880 it was returned to the cathedral.) The interior was painted and gilded, so as to give an accurate picture of what the intended building would look like. Unfortunately, as is made clear elsewhere in this book, the Great Model design was not that finally built: the most obvious differences between the cathedral as we have it and the Model are that the latter has a spectacular single-storey portico of eight fluted columns, and a western vestibule which is covered by an elegant subsidiary dome and lantern.

The lantern supports a stepped pyramidal finial on which is a statue of St Paul, foreshadowing the figure of King George II which was to crown the tower of Hawksmoor's church of St George, Bloomsbury (1716–31). The eastern part of the building is in essence the same form as that of the Greek cross design. The Great Model cost over £500 to make, and is approximately 18 feet (6 metres) long.

Other Furnishings in the Nave of the Crypt
On the north side, close to the Great Model, is the so-called First Model which shows the curious choir of the First Design. The north and south galleries were intended to be raised over arcaded walks opening to the outside of the building, and producing a rather strange-shaped space internally. The lighter-coloured woodwork indicates recent, and skilfully executed, twentieth-century repair work. Also nearby are twentieth-century models of old St Paul's cathedral and the structures immediately associated with it, and of New St Paul's as built.

In a recess on the south side is the tall marble pulpit made for the dome area (for the position which Lord Mottistone's pulpit occupies now). This was designed by F C Penrose, and made 1860–1. The body of the pulpit is hexagonal in shape and of several different-coloured marbles; it is raised high up on twelve slender marble columns with Composite capitals. It was provided as a memorial to Captain Robert Fitzgerald (d. 1853), an officer in the Punjab Frontier Force. A large and interesting photograph nearby not only shows the pulpit in position (with a later tester added) but also the pre-Second World War appearance of the whole choir, dominated by Bodley's towering marble reredos. The frontal on the high altar in this photograph is on display in the Treasury.

An enjoyable but probably little-noticed aspect of the nineteenth-century improvements carried out to the crypt is the mosaic flooring. This was designed by F C Penrose, and carried out in two phases in the 1860s and 1870s, using the enforced craft skills of women convicts from Woking prison. The area covered includes the Wellington tomb-chamber, the cross-aisle to the west of that (in the centre of which is the symbol of the Undivided Trinity), and the central area under the dome which surrounds the sarcophagus of Nelson. The inspiration is Classical, and the workmanship must have been good since it seems to survive the remorseless tread of countless thousands of feet.

Chapter Six

THE MONUMENTS

LIKE WESTMINSTER Abbey, St Paul's is famous for the number and interest of its monuments and memorials. The intention here has been to draw attention to virtually all of them. It has not been possible, however, to be exhaustive: many of the older flat ledger-stones or grave-slabs are difficult to read, for example; and without detailed plans it would be a hard job to identify the positions of many of them; and, moreover, the memorials are still, happily, being added to from time to time; while existing ones are occasionally subject to removal and re-erection in a new position. The Description of the Monuments is, nevertheless, as accurate as it can be at the time of completing the text in September 1986.

There is a useful distinction to be made between monuments which mark the actual place of burial of the person commemorated, and memorials (the two terms are more or less interchangeable) whose purpose is to commemorate or celebrate the memory of a particular individual or group of people. St Paul's has many examples of both but, for obvious reasons, the monuments (whether flat ledger-stones or something more ambitious) connected with burials are all concentrated in the crypt. The last person whose body was buried in St Paul's was Admiral Earl Beatty in 1936; there have been more recent interments of cremated ashes, however.

Sculpture whose purpose is primarily devotional or inspirational, rather than commemorative, has been described under Furnishings and Works of Art. Obvious examples are the two *Mother and Child* sculptures, by Josephina de Vasconcellos and Henry Moore respectively.

There are at least two reasons why burials in the crypt took place fairly early on in the life of the new cathedral. The first was that the parishioners of St Faith-under-St Paul's could still claim the right of burial in the eastern part of the crypt to the same extent that they could have done if their parish church had still been standing: this must be the explanation of a number of the earlier burials recorded, by means of their ledger-stones, in the eastern arm of the crypt. The parishioners of the former church of St Gregory, on the other hand, had a special burial chamber constructed for them; and the entrance to this can still be seen on the south side of the cathedral churchyard.

The other reason was that special exceptions were early on made for people who, on good grounds, had a particular claim to the affection and interest of the cathedral community. They include Wren's daughter, the wife of his son, his sister and brother-in-law (who was, however, a member of the Chapter) and, of course, Wren himself. This group of monuments, close together in the east bay of the south aisle of the crypt, is of wholly exceptional interest both artistically and for their connection with Wren.

As though taking a cue from Wren's presence the crypt became, and has remained, a place for the burial or commemoration (now, only the latter) of distinguished architects, painters, sculptors and writers. This, in itself, makes the crypt a place of pilgrimage for many. Sir Joshua Reynolds, W Holman Hunt, and Sir Alfred Gilbert are just three representative names out of many eighteenth- and nineteenth-century artists; while, in this century, the custom has developed of commemorating successive Presidents of the Royal Academy of Arts by a series of well-mannered (though not always memorable) wall tablets. Because sculpture and letter-cutting are to this day living and thriving arts in England, it is a special pleasure of St Paul's that some of the most recent tablets (e.g. those of Sir Philip Sidney by David Kindersley and Lida Lopes Cardozo and to Ivor Novello by John Skelton) are as much worth looking at as some of the earliest ones.

The carved motif of three winged cherubs' skulls, at the entrance to the staircase leading down into the crypt, suggests that it was intended from the first to serve as a place of burial. But upstairs, at the level of the main floor of the cathedral, the Dean and Chapter originally set their face against allowing a plethora of monuments to disturb the integrity of the architecture. For something like three-quarters of a century there were no monuments at all allowed in the cathedral. Towards the end of the eighteenth century, however, the Dean and Chapter decided to sanction the erection of the four great commemorative statues of Sir Joshua Reynolds (who died in 1792, and is buried in the crypt), Dr Samuel Johnson, John Howard, and Sir William Jones in the diagonal corners of the dome. Three of these are by John Bacon the elder, and one (Reynolds) is by John Flaxman; both will readily be accounted as amongst our ablest Neo-Classical sculptors, even though these (with the possible exception of John Howard's statue, and the relief carving on the plinth) are hardly amongst their most distinguished works. In giving their permission for the first of these, to John Howard, the Dean and Chapter stipulated that 'no monuments should be erected without the design having been first approved by a Committee of the Royal Academy, that nothing might be done that would not correspond with or contribute to the ornament of the building'.

Between 1793 and 1815 the United Kingdom was at war with Napoleonic France: many battles and heroic exploits produced a bumper crop of heroes, and the desirability of commemorating them in a very public and prestigious place. Westminster Abbey had already begun to seem rather overcrowded, and St Paul's was blissfully innocent, for the most part, of commemorative sculpture. And so, within a comparatively short space of time, St Paul's became a rival Valhalla for the nation's honoured dead. In 1796 the Royal Academy established a formal committee to give advice on the erection of these memorials, consisting of three architects (Robert Smirke, James Wyatt, and George Dance the younger), a painter (James Barry) and two sculptors (Thomas Banks and John Bacon the elder). This committee was instrumental in advising on the erection of the commemorative statue to Sir William Jones (by John Bacon) and on the monuments to Captain Burges (by Thomas Banks) and Captain Faulkner (by Rossi) but the results of its efforts were not universally applauded. In 1802 the Treasury therefore appointed its own Committee of National Monuments (popularly known as the 'Committee of Taste', and consisting of grandees and connoisseurs rather than architects and artists) with responsibility for the allocation of public money, choice of artists and designs, selection of sites, size, and payment. Under their aegis the monuments to Lord Howe (by Flaxman) and General Abercromby (Richard Westmacott the younger) were created, and then those to Captain Westcott (by Banks) and to Captains Mosse and Riou (by Rossi).

Between the end of the eighteenth century and 1891, when a Royal Commission was appointed to enquire into the use of Westminster Abbey and St Paul's as places of national commemoration, Parliament was found to have paid for no less than thirty-three substantial memorials to be erected in St Paul's. The most significant from an artistic point of view, and certainly the most expensive from a financial point of view, were those to Lord Rodney, Earl Howe, Sir Ralph Abercromby, Lord Nelson and Marquis Cornwallis which all cost £6,300 apiece. That to Captain Burges (which cost £5,250) was less expensive, but still a major work of sculpture by Thomas Banks. All of them were powerful examples of Neo-Classical taste, and as a group they are even more remarkable than they would be severally. Mrs Katharine Esdaile, an early enthusiast for English eighteenth- and early nineteenth-century sculpture, referred to them collectively as the 'Peninsular School'.

During the mid- and late nineteenth century the custom of commemorating the men and women who had been responsible for the enlargement and maintenance of the British Empire grew; Bishops of London, Deans of St Paul's, and members of the Chapter and of the College of Minor Canons also began increasingly to be commemorated. Giving evidence to the Commission of 1891 the forthright Canon Gregory declared the policy of the Dean and Chapter as it then stood: 'For a long time it has been exceedingly difficult to get consent for any funeral at all. There are certain people who have claimed the right of burial there, such as the minor canons and the virgers, and that right has not been contested; but for the future we should object to it.' On the subject of aesthetic control he replied with equal crispness: 'We absolutely refuse them if they are not satisfactory. We require to see every design, and we have, we believe, absolute authority.'

The most conspicuous monuments in St Paul's are unquestionably those to Wellington (in the middle bay of the north nave arcade) and Nelson (in the middle bay of the south transept). Both lie buried in the crypt, each in a spectacular sarcophagus; and each is still in some sense the object of pilgrimage or curiosity. The most haunting memorial perhaps, and arguably also the most beautiful, is Nicholas Stone's memorial to John Donne, the early seventeenth-century poet and Dean of St Paul's. This is also the only memorial to have

LEFT: *Valour and Cowardice, a detail from the Duke of Wellington's Memorial (no. 214).*
RIGHT: *Britannia commends Nelson's heroism to two schoolboys, a detail from the memorial by Flaxman (no. 249).*

survived the Great Fire unscathed from old St Paul's.

Taken as a whole, the monuments and memorials form a collection of quite exceptional interest, historically and artistically, for which Westminster Abbey offers the only parallel (though perhaps Bath Abbey runs it a close second). That they vary greatly in quality, size and successfulness as commemorative art is part of their attraction. Here is not dull uniformity, though there are a good many family likenesses.

A visit to St Paul's which embraces a steady and thoughtful look at its monuments, upstairs in the church and downstairs in the crypt, will necessarily be, in a very real sense, a progress through British history of the past two hundred and fifty years.

THE CRYPT

There are many possible ways of visiting and enjoying the monuments, but the route followed by this guide is first the crypt, and then the principal floor space of the cathedral.

Entering the crypt from the south transept stair the visitor

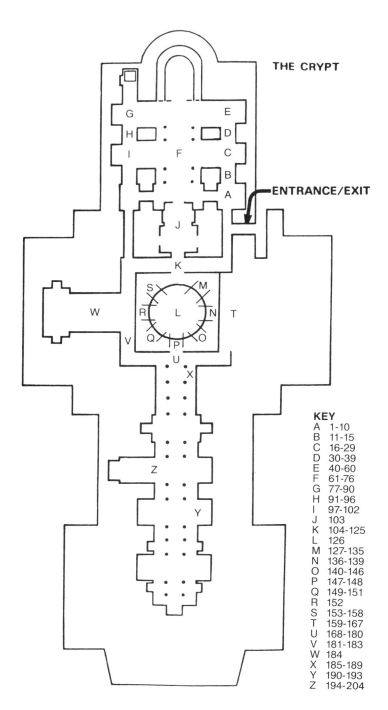

THE CRYPT

ENTRANCE/EXIT

KEY
A 1-10
B 11-15
C 16-29
D 30-39
E 40-60
F 61-76
G 77-90
H 91-96
I 97-102
J 103
K 104-125
L 126
M 127-135
N 136-139
O 140-146
P 147-148
Q 149-151
R 152
S 153-158
T 159-167
U 168-180
V 181-183
W 184
X 185-189
Y 190-193
Z 194-204

126

will first encounter one of the massive foundation piers for the dome. [The tour of the crypt is shown on the plan opposite, and the letters in brackets refer to this.] Turn right into:

South aisle, west bay (A)
Set in the floor are four ledgers, including one to chorister John Howell, d. 1708, 'who from his youth was educated in ye Divine Service of ye Church and bless'd with a Voice suitable to his Employment'.

On the walls (clockwise in every bay, from left to right):

1. Sir Harry Smith Parkes, d. 1885 in Peking, after a distinguished military and diplomatic career in the Far East. Good portrait bust in white marble.

2. Captain Henry Langhorne Thompson, d. 1856 aged 26, 'one of the defenders of Kars'. Tablet incorporating a portrait medallion framed by military trophies. By G G Adams (1821–98), 1860.

3. Captain Alexander Macnab, 'Aide-de-Camp to Lieut. General Sir Thomas Picton who was with him slain at Waterloo' (1815). Plain tablet with lettering characteristic of its time, put up only in 1876.

4. Colonel Sir Duncan MacDougall, d. 1862. After active military service at the Cape, the Spanish Peninsula, France and America, he 'raised the Lancashire Artillery Militia, and was among the first to promote the volunteer movement'. Inscription tablet surmounted by a richly-bearded bust. By G G Adams.

5. John Wasdale, MD, d. 1807. Charming Neo-Classical composition. The verse, which vividly conveys late Georgian religious sentiment, reads:
 'Borne on thy wings, Sweet Hope! on whom I rest,
 My humble Spirit's passport to the Blest,
 From life's delusive, transient joys I rise,
 To seek eternal pleasure in the Skies.'
By Robert Blore of Piccadilly. Father and son, both called Robert, practised as sculptors c. 1790–1835. The ledger below marks the place of burial.

6. Richard Southwell Bourke, Earl of Mayo and a Viceroy of India, d. 1872. A fine marble bust.

7. Magnificent raised ledger to Robert Mylne FRS, d. 1811, architect, who designed Blackfriars Bridge and was Surveyor to the Fabric of St Paul's. 'His remains now repose under the Protection of this Edifice which was so long the object of his Care.'

8. Bishop John Jackson, d. 1885, bishop successively of Lincoln and London. Full-length recumbent effigy, formerly in the south choir aisle, by Thomas Woolner RA 1887. Woolner (d. 1892) was a member of the Pre-Raphaelite Brotherhood.

9. Thomas Bennet, d. 1706, 'Citizon and Stationer'. A fine architectural composition, rather like a reredos, perhaps designed by Wren or someone close to him. Marvellous lettering. The adjoining ledger marks the actual place of burial.

OPPOSITE: Plan of the crypt.

10. Sir John MacDonald, d. 1891.
'A British subject I am born
A British subject I will die.'
This Proconsul was for 19 years
Premier of Canada. Marble bust
on a bracket, a pendant to Lord
Mayo's monument.

South aisle, second bay (B)

11. Edward Bulwer-Lytton, first
Earl of Lytton, d. 1891. Diplomat
and man of letters; Viceroy of
India (1876–80), then Ambassador
to France. Green marble frames a
magnificent sculpture in bronze in
which three other-worldly figures
surround a casket bearing a relief
portrait. By Sir Alfred Gilbert.

12. Admiral Sir James Scott,
d. 1872. Tablet with robust aedi-
cular frame. Not loveable.

13. Sir John Goss, d. 1880. Organist of St Paul's for 34 years, and
a notable composer of church
music. Delicate relief sculpture of
five St Paul's choristers in front of
organ pipes. By J Belcher, RA.

14. Revd William Webber,
d. 1881 in Switzerland. Cultivated, musical minor canon and
sub-dean. His monument is, like
the man, quietly distinguished and
has a white marble portrait relief
in a grey marble surround.

15. Brass tablet to those who died
in the Transvaal 1880–1 during the
Boer Wars.

South aisle, third bay (C)

First a group of ten ledgers, some
of which are becoming difficult to
read on accout of the remorseless
tread of visitors' feet. The most
engaging is to Thomas Cooke 'of
Bobbin in the County of Kent',
d. 1692. Was his one of the first

burials in the new cathedral and, if
so, why?

Historically the most interesting
is to C R Cockerell, d. 1863, distinguished architect and Surveyor
to the Fabric of St Paul's. His wife
Ann was daughter of John Rennie,
whose tomb (No. 29) is next door.
Another is to Mary, wife of Sir
William Robinson of Newby
Park near Ripon in Yorkshire,
d. 1717.

The monuments on the west
return wall on the visitor's left
form a particularly handsome
group, and they are (left to right):

16. Bishop Piers Claughton,
d. 1884. Archdeacon of London
but formerly a Bishop, first of St
Helena and then of Colombo.
Circular portrait relief in three-
quarters profile, a sharp nose and
rather a severe face; set in an
exceptionally rich frame of coloured marbles, pedimented and
scrolled.

17. Maria Hackett, d. 1874 aged
90. A great campaigner for 'the
welfare of cathedral and collegiate
chorister boys'.

18. Revd Benjamin Webb,
d. 1885. A founding father of the
nineteenth-century High Church
movement in the Church of England, and founder-member of the
Cambridge Camden Society (later
the Ecclesiological Society), which
campaigned for the scholarly restoration and refurnishing of
ancient churches, the building of
'ecclesiologically correct' new
ones, and the revival of church
music and liturgy. His monument
shows him three-quarter length in
a niche, and this is but the central
part of a magnificent Italian
Renaissance-style composition.

*OPPOSITE: Bronze relief, detail from Sir Alfred Gilbert's memorial to the first Earl
of Lytton (no. 11).*

He, indeed, looks more like a fifteenth-century Florentine cardinal than a nineteenth-century Anglican priest. By Henry Hugh Armstead RA.

19. Bishop Robert Billing, d. 1898. Bishop of Bedford and suffragan bishop for East and North London. The style is eighteenth-century English Baroque but, curiously, the centrepiece is a portrait painted on stone and surrounded by mosaic.

20. Maria Mary Fussell, d. 1881. Her benefaction of £111,000 (then an immense sum) contributed to the founding of 32 new parishes in London 1883–1903. A sobering thought, in an age when so many parishes have to be amalgamated, and churches closed.

21. Revd Henry Scott Holland, d. 1918. A canon of St Paul's and Regius Professor of Divinity at Oxford. An attenuated alabaster tablet of great beauty, with elegant lettering.

22. Walter de la Mare, OM, CH, d. 1956. Poet and, in his childhood, a St Paul's chorister. Fine example of contemporary lettering, on black slate, designed by the celebrated typographer Berthold Wolpe and cut by John Andrews.

23. E V Knox, 'Poet and satirist, editor of *Punch* 1932–1949'. Fine black slate roundel framed in white freestone. By John Skelton.

24. Revd Henry Venn, d. 1873. A Secretary of the Church Missionary Society. An architectural framework, late Baroque in style, forms the setting for a noble Beethovenian bust—alas unsigned.

25. A large freestone tablet to F C Penrose, 1817–1903, who for 45 years was Surveyor to the Fabric of St Paul's. He was not only an architect but, like Wren, an 'antiquary and astronomer'. Finely lettered.

26. Charles Booth, 1840–1916. Described as 'Merchant and Shipowner', but better known for his researches into and writings on the 'social, industrial and religious condition of the people of London'. Renaissance-style monument; two columns support an entablature with a frieze of seahorses, and over it a shell motif.

27. In the window recess is Sir Francis Chantrey's superb kneeling figure of Bishop Reginald Heber, Bishop of Calcutta, and author of several well-known hymns including 'From Greenland's icy mountains'. He died, aged only 43, in 1826. It is to people like him that we owe the far-flung character of modern Anglicanism. The monument was originally upstairs, and in its present state is incomplete—though well arranged. The figure of the bishop is flanked by a beautiful relief panel showing him confirming young Indian Christians, and the inscription tablet.

28. Sir Edwin Landseer, 1802–73, the painter, by Thomas Woolner RA 1882. A successful monument in which a relief portrait of Landseer is accompanied by a representation of one of his most famous paintings, *The Shepherd's Mourner*. Above are his pallet and brushes, and to the sides the inevitable lions. Landseer designed the lions for the monument to Lord Nelson in Trafalgar Square.

29. On the floor the robust red granite tomb of John Rennie, 1761–1821, the famous engineer. Beautifully cut lettering: the

inscription seeks to record chiefly his 'private virtues' but cannot resist adding at the end 'Waterloo and Southwark bridges, Plymouth breakwater, Sheerness docks, &c., &c., &c.'

South aisle, fourth bay (D)

Three ledgers, the eastern one indecipherable, the second to Canon Henry Melvill d. 1871, an outstanding preacher, and the third—a minor masterpiece—is:

30. Sir Lawrence Alma-Tadema, 1836–1912, the painter. Rich and sombre, this is a ledger which brilliantly combines black marble with an inscription tablet, border, and relief sculpture in brass. Over the inscription two mourning *putti* with staves support a medallion in which is an upturned torch, a symbol of the snuffing-out of life.

31. Colonel Sir Vivian Dering Majendie, d. 1898. A charming small tablet. Above the inscription three winged cherubs' heads (more like fairies than cherubs) in a technique combining painting and mosaic work.

32. Melton Prior, 1845–1910. Artist and war correspondent for the *Illustrated London News* in thirteen far-flung campaigns. Fine relief portrait in bronze by Bertha Burleigh (1911), bespectacled and in uniform, within an alabaster surround.

33. Sir William Russell, 1820–1907. Described as 'first and greatest of war correspondents', he made his reputation with his reporting of the Crimean War in the 1850s. A lively bronze bust, showing him with notebook and pencil in hand.

34. Wide bronze plaque with a mourning female figure in low relief, set in a red marble frame, recording the names and newspapers of thirteen special correspondents who lost their lives in the South African War 1899–1902. A sober reminder that journalism can be a dangerous profession in troubled times and places. By Sir William Goscombe John, RA.

35. Revd John Vidgen Povah, d. 1882. Forty-nine years a minor canon. An off-the-peg brass plaque by T Pratt and Sons.

36. Archibald Forbes, 1838–1900. War correspondent and military historian. Bronze relief portrait, lettering, and frame in a green marble setting. By H Charles Fehr.

37. Brass plaque with relief portrait and engraved landscape of the sun setting beyond a broad stretch of river to Lt Colonel James Grant, 1827–92, who 'in company with Speke discovered the source of the Nile 1860–3'.

38. Large brass plaque designed by Herbert Johnson and engraved by Gawthorp, full of interest visually, to seven special correspondents who lost their lives in the Sudan in 1883–5. The scene at the top shows a correspondent in the thick of battle, recording it all; at the foot six little graves with crosses in an uncompromising landscape.

39. Brass plaque with large solemn black and red Latin inscription to Revd George How, d. 1893, a prebendary and a vigorous parish priest.

South aisle, fifth bay (E)

Here the ledgers present a special group, for there are seventeen altogether, and three are of parti-

*LEFT: Marble relief, detail from Belcher's memorial to Sir John Goss (no. 13).
RIGHT: Francis Bird's tender relief carving on the memorial to Wren's daughter, Jane
(no. 52).*

cular interest as works of art in their own right. Nor are the others without interest, including two fine early black marble ledgers to Elizabeth Wiseman, d. 1694, and John de la Fontaine of Kerby Bellars, Leicestershire, d. 1708; and Landseer's grave-slab (as opposed to his monument, No. 28). Others (working from west to east, anticlockwise) are to George Dawe, d. 1829, 'historical and portrait painter'; Henry Fuseli RA, d. 1825, another specialist in historical painting, and of much more than passing interest (his ledger tells us also that he was born in Zurich and died in Putney Hill); George Dance the younger, d. 1825, not only an architect of great ability (All Hallows, London Wall 1767; Newgate Prison

1770–80, demolished 1902) but also a fine artist, and the last to survive of the 'Original Forty Royal Academicians'; Benjamin West, a notable early nineteenth-century painter and President of the Royal Academy (a large and magnificent altarpiece by him can be seen hanging on the north wall of St Stephen Walbrook in the City), b. Pennsylvania 1738 and d. 1820 in London; J M W Turner RA, painter (whose monument is in the south transept, above), d. 1851; James Barry, d. 1806, another 'history painter' and the artist who decorated the lecture theatre of the Royal Society of Arts in London; Sir Joshua Reynolds, 1723–92, another President of the Royal Academy and one of the greatest portrait painters of all time (there is, surely, an argument for recutting his inscription before it disappears?); John Opie RA, painter, d. 1807; William Holman Hunt OM, 1827–1910, the Pre-Raphaelite painter whose *Light of the World* painting hangs in the cathedral (his is a typical subtly-designed ledger by Eric Gill, with beautiful heraldry); and William Hoare, citizen and cordwainer, d. 1808.

The three of particular artistic merit are those to Boehm, Leighton and Millais. Boehm's ledger is on the inner side of the bay, west of the tablet to Blake; the other two are close to the window bay.

40. Sir Joseph Edgar Boehm RA, 1834–90, sculptor. His ledger is wholly of brass, in a black marble frame, and is signed Elkington & Co. It is becoming badly worn.

41. Frederic Leighton (Lord Leighton), 1830–96. A great nineteenth-century painter and President of the Royal Academy. His monument is upstairs but here he lies under a sumptuous brass ledger designed by Richard Norman Shaw RA depicting, in vigorous relief, his coat of arms and a sprig of weeping willow.

42. Sir John Everett Millais, 1829–96, Pre-Raphaelite painter and President of the Royal Academy. Superb combination of black marble and brass, also designed by the architect Richard Norman Shaw, RA. Above the noble lettering of the inscription a wreath encircles his coat of arms.

Returning to the walls, we follow clockwise:

43. George Richmond RA, 1809–96. Notable painter, and father of Sir William Richmond who designed the scheme of mosaic decoration for the choir. Within a dark red marble frame with Renaissance ornament is an inscription in raised lettering—not common in St Paul's—and above a bronze relief portrait flanked by two masculine mourning angels. By Sir William Richmond, KCB, RA.

44. Freestone Classical tablet to four members of the cathedral staff who died in the First World War 1914–19. Presumably designed by Sir Mervyn Macartney, Surveyor to the Fabric. Beneath, a tablet to two of their successors who died in the Second World War.

45. Sir Anthony Van Dyck, d. 1641 at Blackfriars and buried in old St Paul's. Large freestone monument in Baroque style, with broken pediment framing a portrait bust. By H Poole RA, 1928. The bronze wreath below is a tribute from Van Dyck's native city of Antwerp.

46. Sir Aston Webb, 1849–1930. Architect and President of the Royal Academy. Freestone, portrait in relief.

47. Sir Frank Dicksee, 1853–1928. President of the Royal Academy. Plain stone tablet with moulded surround.

48. Sir William Llewellyn PRA, 1863–1941. Freestone, and the best of this group of three. A wreath encircles the main inscription, but a pleasant feature is the raised lettering round the square frame.

49. William Blake, 1757–1827. Artist, poet, and mystic. Large rectangular freestone tablet with a portrait relief, not very good. Fortunately he has a memorial bust by Sir Jacob Epstein in Westminster Abbey. By H Poole RA, 1927.

50. Mary, d. 1712, first wife of Christopher Wren, son of Sir Christopher. A small masterpiece of its genre. The inscription is contained within a vigorously carved cartouche, rising to a climax near the top with two *putti* (one with hour-glass) and the shield of arms. Which of his master craftsmen could Wren have asked to carve this handsome piece, which also seems invested with real feeling?

51. Edmund Wiseman, d. 1704. Was he a friend of Wren's? Below a marble pediment an oval-framed inscription panel wreathed in fruit and flowers. At the top are two winged cherubs, at the foot two winged skulls. A work of high quality. Mrs Wiseman's fine black ledger is below in the floor.

52. Rectangular marble panel, the frame richly carved with acanthus leaves and enclosing a high relief sculpture of a young woman playing the organ and surrounded by *putti*. This is Francis Bird's monument to Wren's daughter, Jane, who died in 1702 aged 26: a fine and poignant work of memorial art.

53. William Hoare, d. 1808. Modest Greek-Revival tablet.

54. Randolph Caldecott, 1846–86. 'An artist whose sweet and dainty grace has not been in its kind surpassed, whose humour was as quaint as it was inexhaustible.' This is one of the strangest and most beautiful works of art in the cathedral, and one of the most memorable. It is by Sir Alfred Gilbert of 'Eros' (Piccadilly) fame. Within an attenuated granite aedicule, supported by bronze columns, is a painted metal sculpture of a tenderly mourning child, holding a relief medallion of the artist. The child wears an elaborate, and typically Gilbertian, head-dress.

55. Brass plaque, in cartouche form on black marble, to Sir Joseph Edgar Boehm, RA, the first sculptor to be created a baronet, d. 1890. By Elkington and Co.

Almost all the remaining monuments in this bay are to members of the Wren family, a fitting climax for those visitors who lack the time or stamina to explore the other monuments of the crypt in detail.

56. Revd Dr William Holder, d. 1697, and his wife Susanna (Wren's sister) d. 1688. A fine Baroque double-monument, the inscription panels flanked by winged *putti* who hold aside draperies; above, a shower of roses emerges from the draperies. His inscription is in Latin, as befits a man of learning who was also a canon of St Paul's; hers is in English, and records that Susanna 'applied herself to the knowledge of Medicinal Remidies . . .' to such good effect that 'thousands were happily healed by her and no one ever miscarried'.

57. Constantia Wren, d. 1851 aged 93, Wren's great grand-daughter. Attractive white marble tablet, framed by draperies and bearing the Wren shield of arms. Below her tablet is Constantia's grave-slab, modelled on Wren's own just to the west of hers.

58. Wren's grave-slab is an immense piece of black marble 6 in. (15 cm) thick, on short legs, with a simple inscription in large Roman lettering recording that 'Here Lieth Sr Christopher Wren Kt the Builder of this Cathedral Church of ST. PAUL, &c., who Dyed in

LEFT: *Painted aluminium figure of a child, detail from Sir Alfred Gilbert's memorial to Randolph Caldecott (no. 54).*
RIGHT: *Ivor Novello, by John Skelton (no. 70).*

the Year of our LORD MDCCXXIII, and of his Age XCI.' Above it on the wall is a rectangular white marble inscription panel, in which the lettering is of positively antique magnificence and framed by deeply-cut egg and dart motif. The inscription is in Latin and concludes with the famous injunction 'Lector, si monumentum requiris, circumspice'. ('Reader, if you seek a memorial: look around you.') Rarely, if ever, has anything been better said.

59. Below is a discreet twentieth-century tablet with relief sculpture of masons' tools, erected by the Worshipful Company of Masons, to 'the men who made shapely the stones of St Paul's cathedral 1675–1708'. Although well-intentioned, the tablet disturbs the noble simplicity of Wren's own.

60. James Barry, RA, d. 1806 (his ledger is mentioned earlier). Here he is commemorated by a fine Coade (i.e. patent artificial) stone bust of 1818, and an inscription praising him as both writer and painter and as one who had 'a moral tendency and a Grecian taste', certainly an unusual combination.

In this eastern part of the crypt (**F**), still known as St Faith-under-St Paul's but also dedicated as the Chapel of the Most Excellent Order of the British Empire, the apsidal east end and its ambulatories are sensibly kept free of monuments. The tour of the monuments continues by treating the 'nave' of the chapel as a single space and moving round it clockwise, and then up the north aisle westwards, bay by bay.

First the ledgers. Of these there are a considerable number, and not all of them readily accessible, but those of particular note are to Thomas Felsted, d. 1711 (for its fine lettering); Very Revd Robert Gregory (d. 1911) Dean of St Paul's; Very Revd Henry Milman (d. 1868), another great nineteenth-century Dean; Mary Knight (d. 1773) again for its marvellous lettering; and others: Canon Henry Liddon (d. 1890), a sumptuous brass ledger with romanesque-style ornament designed by Bodley and Garner; Major General Sir Ino: Brathwaite (d. 1803) with its inscription like a copper-plate engraving; and that to Alexander Wedderburn, d. 1805, Earl of Rosslyn, a ferocious judge at the time of the Gordon Riots (1780), who gave his name to Rosslyn Hill and Wedderburn Road in Hampstead. On the north side is a notable group of musicians, including William Boyce (d. 1779) and Sir Hubert Parry (d. 1918), the composer of 'Blest pair of sirens' and the well-known setting of Blake's *Jerusalem*.

61. Ledger to Sir Edward Poynter PRA, 1836–1919. A painter, teacher and Director of the National Gallery, who had great artistic influence in his lifetime. Another example of the sumptuous combination of black marble and brass, with a shield of arms in relief. Signed AMP.

62. Wall tablet to Sir Hamo Thornycroft RA, 1850–1925.

Sculptor. Bronze relief portrait on a discreetly Classical marble tablet. Signed C L Hartwell RA.

63. Sir William Reid Dick RA, 1878–1961. Sculptor. Good in its strong simplicity, an object lesson indeed.

64. Sir George Frampton RA, 1860–1928. A most engaging memorial. Freestone niche in which is placed a bronze *putto* holding a miniature representation of Frampton's *Peter Pan* in Kensington Gardens. By Ernest Gillick ARA and HCB.

65. Sir Alfred Gilbert RA, sculptor, 1854–1934. Also good: bronze oval relief of a figure of Eros, though not copying Gilbert's own celebrated sculpture. By Gilbert Ledward RA, 1937.

66. Sir Edwin Lutyens OM, 1869–1944. Architect and President of the Royal Academy. Freestone tablet and shield of arms in coloured metals. Lacks the visual distinction of its neighbours. Designed by W Curtis Green RA, 1946.

67. Sir Max Beerbohm, 1872–1956. Caricaturist and writer. A pendant to Reid Dick's, and with the same virtues.

68. Canon William Newbolt, 1844–1930. Simple elegant Renaissance-style tablet with excellent lettering, of alabaster.

69. Tablets, large and small, to members of the Amen Court Guild who died in the First and Second World Wars respectively. How not to do it.

70. Ivor Novello, 1893–1951. Composer. Everything about this

OPPOSITE: John Singer Sargent's deeply felt bronze Crucifixion, given by his sisters as his own memorial (no. 75).

IN MEMORIAM
JOHN SINGER SARGENT, R.A. 1856-1925.
THIS WORK OF HIS HANDS, PRESENTED BY HIS SISTERS,
WAS ERECTED BY THE ROYAL ACADEMY OF ARTS.

monument is good—the stilted oval shape, the colour and texture of the stone, the delicate relief portrait, the lettering and the colour it is painted, and the beautiful quotation: 'Blaze of lights and music calling, Music weeping, rising, falling, like a rare and precious diamond His brilliance still lives on.' By John Skelton.

71. Sir Stafford Cripps, 1889–1952. An admirable bronze half-figure on a grey marble base with an inscription which gives us the measure of the man: 'If man neglects the things of the spirit and puts aside the full armour of God he will seal the doom of future generations.' By Sir Jacob Epstein, 1954. Stafford Cripps was a man of vision, in his private as well as in his public life as Chancellor of the Exchequer. His village, Filkins, in Oxfordshire, is a model of how an extremely attractive village can be successfully enlarged without aesthetic loss; and he set up the National Heritage Memorial Fund, to which we owe so much.

72. John Wyclif, d. 1384. A new (1986) slate oval tablet to a theologian who inspired the first complete translation of the Bible into English. By Mark Bury.

73. Gordon Hamilton-Fairley, 1930–75. First professor of medical oncology. Killed by a terrorist bomb in London. Circular slate tablet with good lettering. By Richard Kindersley.

74. Sir Alexander Fleming FRS, 1881–1955. Discoverer of penicillin. White marble tablet with a border of thistles. It could have been done a hundred years earlier.

75. John Singer Sargent RA, 1856–1925. It comes as something of a surprise to find that the dazzlingly brilliant and successful painter of fashionable late Victorian and Edwardian portraits could also create such a deeply-felt religious work as this great bronze sculpture of Christ on the cross. The imagery is powerful and original: Christ is shown at the moment of fulfilment, Redemption achieved, his face drained of energy yet strangely eloquent. Beneath his outstretched arms a man and a woman are crouched, and they hold chalices beneath his pierced hands. Christ's legs and feet straddle and, as it were, contain the serpent of evil. The text 'Remissa sunt peccata mundi' ('The sins of the world are forgiven') appears by Christ's head. At the foot of the cross the pelican, type of Christ, wounds its breast to feed its young. It is a very personal and unexpected memorial, given by his sisters.

76. Sir Arthur Sullivan, d. 1900, composer of church music and collaborator with W S Gilbert on the series of operas which have made them, as 'Gilbert and Sullivan', household names. A beautiful brass ledger, which has a wide border of birds in foliage; the central panel has the inscription in fine raised Art Nouveau-ish lettering, a spray of leaves, and the lyre as a symbol of musical composition.

North aisle, first bay (G) (each bay clockwise)

There are approximately a dozen ledgers in this bay, largely indecipherable.

77. Canon John Collins, d. 1982. Founder of Christian Action and a founder of the Campaign for Nuclear Disarmament. It is fitting

that this courageous Christian, admirable preacher and contemporary prophet should have a memorial in St Paul's, and that the fine lettering should be the work of Tony Webb, the cathedral's present-day master carver.

78. Martha Coby, d. 1707. A large oval with bolection moulding, and of interest for two reasons: it is in the lifetime of Wren, who may have designed it or approved it, and its deeply-cut characters are the epitome of what good lettering should be like.

79. Sir Thomas Monnington, PRA, 1902–76. Painter. Rectangular tablet of polished limestone with rounded top enclosing portrait relief. An example of late twentieth-century reticence and good manners by Willi Soukop RA, 1980.

80. Alderman John Norton, Master of the Worshipful Company of Stationers, who (as the twentieth-century inscription says) in 1612 provided a benefaction to provide an Ash Wednesday preacher 'yearly for ever' for St Faith-under-St Paul's.

81. Sir Joseph Simpson, d. 1968. Commissioner of Police for London. White marble tablet, with relief portrait showing a strong character. By John Skelton.

82. Sir Percy Sillitoe, d. 1962. Small marble tablet with shield of arms.

83. Felix Johnson, d. 1918. Rectangular alabaster tablet.

84. Jonathan Battishill, 1738–1801. His anthem 'The Lord looked down from Heaven' is still sung in cathedrals. Nos 82–4 all commemorate former choristers.

85. Francis Holl RA, d. 1888, painter. His monument is rather an ambitious one, well placed in a deep window recess. Renaissance-style framework with an alert bronze bust by Sir Alfred Gilbert in a shell-headed niche.

86. Henry Liddon, d. 1890, canon of St Paul's and a 'silver-tongued' preacher. White marble effigy on a black marble plinth, now in a window recess but originally upstairs.

87. John Martin, d. 1680. Printer. A fine Baroque monument, of the type with a tomb-chest and a reredos-like architectural back-drop with segmental pediment and cartouche. On the tomb-chest John Martin and his wife kneel either side of a table on which is heaped a neat pyramidal pile of printed books.

88. W R Matthews (d. 1974), Dean of St Paul's during the Second World War. Freestone tablet with good lettering by David Kindersley.

89. Martin Sullivan (d. 1980), Dean of St Paul's. Slightly smaller freestone tablet with good lettering, also by David Kindersley.

90. W R Inge (d. 1954). Dean of St Paul's during the First World War and until 1934. Unusually, his quietly distinguished monument with its shaped frame and its relief portrait was given by his publishers.

North aisle, second bay (H)
91. Sir Charles Wheeler, 1892–1974. Sculptor and PRA. Of the same type as Monnington and Kelly. By Willi Soukop RA, 1977.

92. Sir William Quiller Orchardson RA, 1835–1910, painter. An intriguing monument: against a

black marble backdrop with swept-up gable is placed a miniature Neo-Classical tomb with an urn, and flanking this are small gilt-bronze sculptures of Britannia and Napoleon (a reference to his painting of *The Relief of the Bellerophon*) by Sir William Reynolds-Stephens RA.

93. Edwin Austin Abbey RA, 1852–1911. Elegant bronze tablet in Art Nouveau-Baroque style to an American mural painter who settled in England and left a substantial sum of money to the Royal Academy for commissioning large works of art in public buildings.

94. Sir Gerald Kelly, d. 1972, PRA. By David McFall RA, 1973.

95. Sir John Dykes Bower, d. 1981. Organist of St Paul's for 31 years. Designed in a late seventeenth-century style, with good deeply-cut lettering, by his brother Stephen Dykes Bower, who designed the baldacchino and high altar of St Paul's.

96. Sir George Martin, d. 1916. Organist of St Paul's for 28 years. Bronze portrait medallion on a background of two different-coloured marbles, all carefully considered in their effect. By Henry Pegram, 1917.

North aisle, third bay (I)
The ledgers include two Late Georgian ones to members of the Rivington family, and otherwise (though numerous) are difficult to read or undistinguished.

97. Sir Alfred Munnings, d. 1959, a notable PRA. Portrait medallion over a small inscription tablet, and enjoyable. Designed to complement No 99.

98. Sir Albert Richardson, d. 1954, PRA, known as 'The Professor', and a man to whom we owe much for his passion for good design, his courage and initiative as an early 'preservationist', and as architect and teacher. He lived the life of a Neo-Georgian, wore eighteenth-century costume at home, and read by candlelight. Bronze portrait medallion on a freestone marble tablet with really excellent lettering. He would have loved it. By Marshall Sisson RA, 1972.

99. John Constable, RA, d. 1837. One of the most cherished of all English painters, he is buried in Hampstead churchyard and his tablet (characteristic of the informed good taste of its time) was put here in 1937. By Alfred Turner RA.

100. Philip Wilson Steer OM, d. 1942. Painter. Freestone tablet carved with cornucopia of flowers and ribbons. Not as bold as the carving of Wren's time, but sympathetic to it.

101. Sir Mervyn Macartney FSA, d. 1932. He was Surveyor to the Fabric of St Paul's from 1906–31, during the crucial repairs of the dome piers from 1925 onwards. He was also a founder of that wonderful body the Art Workers Guild, so many of whose members are commemorated or represented by their work in this eastern part of the crypt.

102. Sir Muirhead Bone RA, d. 1953. Etcher, draughtsman and painter. Gilt lettering on black marble. Good.

West of the Chapel of the Most Excellent Order of the British Empire is an arcade, and west of that again a large chamber (J) in which reposes:

103. The sarcophagus of Arthur Wellesley, first Duke of Wellington, 1769–1852, whose spectacular monument is in the north nave arcade (No 214). But here the great commander lies and, in spite of the bright lighting demanded by modern tourism, the atmosphere of this mausoleum-chamber is very powerful. The sarcophagus of 1858 is austerely Neo-Classical, of red polished Cornish porphyry with gilt lettering, and rests on a plinth of sleeping lions in unpolished white granite. Designed by Penrose, and by him also the standard candleholders in all four corners and the magnificent mosaic floor. A recent addition of real distinction—on account of their spacious layout, good lettering, and congruity of purpose—has been the memorial tablets to Field Marshals who were leaders of the Military Forces of the British Commonwealth of Nations in the Second World War 1939–45 (Alexander of Tunis, Slim, Montgomery, Gort, Auchinleck, Alanbrooke, Wavell, Dill, Wilson, Ironside). The dedication plaques and three tablets are by John Skelton and other tablets are signed by Jack Trowbridge, Paul Wehrle, Helen Bicknell and John Poole.

Turning westwards brings the visitor into a cross aisle (**K**), and a view in the middle distance of Nelson's sarcophagus (No 126). The floors here are again inlaid with mosaic designed by Penrose, in the style of the Italian Renaissance.

In this cross aisle the immediate focus of contemporary attention is the memorial to the South Atlantic Task Force but, as before, a clock-wise order will be adopted.

104. Arthur Thruston of the Oxfordshire Light Infantry, d. 1897. Murdered by mutineers of the Uganda Rifles, whom he approached in circumstances of singular heroism. In an early seventeenth-century Renaissance style, made of alabaster and various marbles.

105. A dignified tablet of polished limestone to members of the Palestine Police Force who died during the British Mandate 1920–48.

106. A memorial tablet and book, in both of which the lettering is excellent, to men and women 'representing many nations' who gave their lives in the Second World War serving in the Air Transport Auxiliary.

107. Professor Edward Palmer, Captain William Gill and Lieutenant Harold Charrington, d. 1882 in the Wady Sadr in the Sinai Desert where they were 'treacherously and cruelly slain', together with two faithful attendants. This poignant testimony to the risks attendant on nineteenth-century scholars, empire-builders and explorers is on a fine handsomely-lettered brass plate of considerable size mounted on marble.

108. The nineteenth- and early twentieth-century memorials in metal in St Paul's would make a study in themselves. This one, in reserved Italian Renaissance style, is to Admiral Sir Harry Rawson, 1843–1910, who captured Benin in 1897.

109. Revd William Nelson DD (Earl Nelson) d. 1835. White marble tablet to a multi-titled clergyman who owed this distinction to the fact that he was Nelson's brother.

110. A large tablet by David

Kindersley in Cumbrian slate to the 255 servicemen, including Captain H Jones VC, who died in the South Atlantic, April–June 1982. A place of pilgrimage for many. In its austere Classical simplicity lies a strange eloquence. The blue-green colour of the slate is sympathetic to the mosaic floor.

111. Sir Charles MacGregor, b. Agra 1840 and d. Cairo 1887. A soldier and a hero of Empire. His bust, which shows him in uniform with twirling moustaches is not, perhaps, one of the most distinguished in the crypt. The bust is supported on a bracket of books representing his literary works, and on the inscription panel a figure of a woman in high relief kneels pensively in mourning. By S. Albano of Florence, 1889.

112. Sir John Eardley Wilmot Inglis, 1814–62. Well worth studying for its careful combination of materials, bronze and three different marbles, and its overall artistic quality. The bronze portrait medallion and relief panel of Lucknow are signed by Francis Derwent Wood 1896, and the memorial as a whole by Seth Smith.

113. Dignified well-lettered tablet to members of the Royal Irish Constabulary who died in war and on duty 1836–1922.

114. Frederick Jackson, d. 1938. Commander of the Jackson-Harmsworth Polar Expedition 1894–7 and rescuer of Dr Nansen. Bronze panel in high relief shows him amidst the icy wastes.

115. Large Italian Renaissance-style monument to Sir William Curzon Wyllie, assassinated in 1909 (but in London not in India,

where he served with great distinction). The portrait relief does not live up to the high standard of the design and well-considered lettering.

116. Field Marshal Lord Strathnairn, 1801–85. Large brass tablet on marble by Frank Smith & Co and not, alas, of artistic merit.

117. A noble freestone memorial in the style of Wren, with a bronze relief of excellent quality of a soldier on horseback, to members of the Middlesex Companies of Imperial Yeomanry who died in the South African War 1900–2. Could it have been designed by Macartney or Lutyens? Side panels and a small pendant below added later.

118. Another memorial to those who died in the South African War, from the Royal Dragoons. Eighteenth-century English Baroque in style, of black and white marble.

119. Rainy Anderson, d. 1901 in action in the Transvaal. By Caffin of Regent Street. The white marble tablet incorporates a relief medallion, his helmet, sword and belt, on a background of black marble.

120. White marble tablet with high relief sculpture of the Angel of Mortality, by Percival Ball, to officers of the Punjab Frontier Force who died in the Afghanistan War of 1878–80.

121. Sir Samuel Browne, 1824–1901. White marble. An Indian figure holds an inscription scroll, and a wreath of mourning. By Forsyth, 1903.

122. Colonel John Gurwood, d. 1845, and the compiler of the

OPPOSITE: Marble relief of Florence Nightingale tending a wounded soldier, detail of no. 124.

Duke of Wellington's despatches who also 'led the forlorn hope to Ciudad Rodrigo'. Minimal Baroque in grey and white marble, with a nice portrait in relief.

123. Octagonal memorial, brass on marble, to two brothers of the Queen's Own Corps of Guides who d. 1857 (Lt. Quintin Battye, before Delhi) and 1879 (Major Wigram Battye, in Afghanistan) respectively.

Before entering the central space below the dome there are two memorials to pause and examine:

124. Florence Nightingale OM, 1820–1910, the codifier and improver of the great tradition of British nursing, who transformed the care of the sick and wounded in the Crimean War. Large Baroque-style frame in marmalade-coloured marble, enclosing a relief sculpture by A G Walker RA.

125. Field Marshal Lord Gort, 1886–1946. A circular memorial of distinction, owing to the fine placing and character of the lettering: it shows what can be achieved, on quite a small scale, in memorial art. By Michael Harvey.

One then approaches (**L**):

126. The sarcophagus of Lord Nelson. Superbly sited in the central space within a ring of eight columns, this elegant sarcophagus which is now the resting place of Britain's most celebrated naval hero was originally made in 1524–9 by Benedetto da Rovezzano for Cardinal Wolsey's tomb at Windsor but was confiscated by Henry VIII. The cardinal lies buried, somewhere, in Leicester and a

viscount's coronet is placed where a cardinal's hat was intended.

From here we again go clockwise in a circle of heroes, this time naval (**M**):

127. Sir Henry Jackson, Admiral of the Fleet 1855–1929. Freestone tablet with a border such as Wren might have indicated, by F G Knapp.

128. Sir John Hawley, 1829–85, who became Governor of Newfoundland. Pedimented Neo-Classical frame, on which is placed a rather ponderous bust.

129. Sir Charles Madden, Admiral of the Fleet, 1862–1935. An excellent example of 1930s good taste by Eric Gill, ARA.

130. Earl Jellicoe, Admiral of the Fleet, 1859–1935, who commanded the Grand Fleet in the crucial period of 1914–16 and was Governor-General of New Zealand in the early 1920s. A noble raised ledger by M Wrightson, with good lettering and well-carved shield of arms.

131. Earl Beatty, Admiral of the Fleet, 1871–1936. Another First World War naval commander. Its studied simplicity deserves careful contemplation.

132. Sir Roger Keyes MP, first Baron Keyes of Zeebrugge and Dover Admiral of the Fleet, 1872–1945. Well-designed wall-tablet with good lettering and shield of arms.

133. Admiral Lord Beresford, 1846–1919. White marble with a good relief portrait in an oval medallion. By John Tweed.

134. Admiral Sir Edward Cod-

OPPOSITE: *Nelson's sarcophagus was originally made for Cardinal Wolsey in 1524–9 (no. 126)*

rington, 1770–1851, conspicuous for his role in the battle of Navarino (1827). The memorial, which incorporates a very solid-looking portrait relief, was not put up until 1884 and is by Albert Bruce Joy.

135. Sir Frederick Richards, Admiral of the Fleet, 1833–1912; Baroque-style frame in alabaster, and white marble portrait relief by Frederick Pomeroy.

In bay two (**N**) we have:

136. Sir Philip Vian, Admiral of the Fleet, 1894–1968. An outstanding naval commander in the Second World War. Fine circular tablet with gilt lettering.

137. Sir Dudley Pound, First Sea Lord, 1877–1943. Rectangular, good lettering also.

138. Large tomb-chest of Cuthbert, Lord Collingwood, Admiral of the Fleet, d. 1810, whose memorial is upstairs.

139. Viscount Cunningham of Hyndhope, Admiral of the Fleet, 1883–1963. Rectangular slate tablet, well achieved.

In bay three (**O**) we have, in addition to a fine mosaic floor, the following monuments:

140. Field Marshal Sir Henry Norman, 1826–1904. Yet another example of artistic distinction being achieved by economy of means: inscription in raised lettering within oval frame, set in a Baroque-style tablet with volutes, and all cast in metal.

141. Lord Napier of Magdala, 1810–90, Field Marshal. A beautiful flat tomb-slab of grey marble, raised on brackets. The design incorporates a cross and lotus leaf ornament. Behind it is Lord Napier's wall memorial. In the Greek-Revival taste, pedimented with acroteria, and made of grey-blue marble somewhat darker than the tomb-slab. There is a portrait relief roundel by Frederick Woodington ARA, 1891, and the inscription panel below records not only Napier's battle honours but also his 'more peaceful achievements: Darjeeling laid out, Umballa created, and the Punjab restored to Peace and Prosperity'.

142. Sir Robert Montgomery, 1809–87. Governor of the Punjab. Portrait relief in white marble, simply but effectively framed. By Albert Bruce Joy.

143. Sir Donald Stewart, 1860–1905, of the Gordon Highlanders. Compare with 140. Bronze tablet, raised lettering, and given visual quality by the design of the border and corner rosettes.

144. Field Marshal Sir John Simmons, 1821–1903. Royal Engineers. Portrait relief showing the bewhiskered soldier full-frontal, which is unusual. Border of oak leaves and acorns.

145. Sir Patrick Grant, 1804–95. Field Marshal. After a military career in India he was Governor of Wren's Royal Hospital in Chelsea. Relief portrait medallion with bay leaves and Field Marshal's baton. By F Verheyden.

146. Sir Donald Stewart, 1824–1900. Field Marshal. Served in India, Abyssinia and Afghanistan and also became Governor of the Royal Hospital. Shield of arms over inscription panel, below which is his baton and sword.

Bay four (**P**) (facing westwards) contains just two large monuments, originally upstairs, and rather over-large in scale here:

147. Captain George Duff, who died in the Battle of Trafalgar (1805). By one of the best Neo-Classical sculptors of that time, John Bacon junior, and paid for by Parliament (£1,575). Over the superbly lettered inscription panel is a sarcophagus with portrait medallion. On the left is Britannia, who pensively arranges a wreath of oak leaves and acorns over the sarcophagus; on the right a midshipman kneels, disconsolately.

148. Captain John Cooke, died at Trafalgar. He commanded the *Bellerophon*, Duff the *Mars*. By Sir Richard Westmacott RA and also paid for by Parliament. A female allegorical figure kneels on one knee, lost in sadness at the thought of victory so dearly achieved. This noble effect is somewhat mitigated by the two *putti*, one of whom sports a trident and the other tries on Victory's helmet at a rakish angle.

Bay five (**Q**) contains two portrait busts of outstanding interest to visitors:

149. George Washington, 1732–99. First President of the United States of America. Bronze portrait bust on a tapering marble plinth, the bust by Droway Partridge. The bust is good, and well-sited visually in relation to the Nelson sarcophagus; yet somewhat tucked away, and seemingly little known.

150. T E Lawrence, 1888–1935, known as 'Lawrence of Arabia'. Bronze bust by Eric Kennington RA showing him with his characteristic hairlick. The bust is on a polished limestone bracket, with an inscription—eloquent, like Lord Beatty's, in its simplicity—in raised polished brass letters.

151. A polished limestone tablet, with subtly curving top, to those who died at the siege of Kut-el-Amara in 1916. Good lettering. A moving reminder, as it was meant to be.

Bay six (**R**) contains only:

152. The massive plain tomb-chest of William du Carl of Northesk, 1758–1831. Admiral of the Fleet and third in command at Trafalgar.

Bay seven (**S**):

153. General Sir Ian Hamilton, 1853–1947. Vaguely Classical marble tablet with gilt lettering.

154. Viscount Wolseley, 1843–1913, Field Marshal. Black marble tablet with superb acanthus-leaf border, shield of arms, and raised lettering, all in gilt metal. Behind such distinction must lie the hand of a really good designer, presumably Sir Mervyn Macartney, the then Surveyor to the Fabric. The plain ledger records the place where Wolseley and his wife lie buried.

155. Sir Henry Wilson, Field Marshal, b. 1864 and murdered (as the ledger nearby records) outside his London home in 1922. Plain black marble cross.

156. Earl Roberts, VC, Field Marshal, 1832–1914. Plain black marble cross with inscription panel attached saying, rather bleakly, 'Roberts'. Associated hardly legible ledger by Eric Gill, ARA.

157. Field Marshal Evelyn Wood, VC, 1838–1919. His career embraced first the navy and then the army. White marble tablet with handsome lettering and with border of acanthus and papyrus leaves.

158. Lt General Lord Freyberg, VC, 1889–1963. Governor General of New Zealand 1945–52. This is one of the more distinguished recent memorials. The lettering has personality, and is balanced by a fully tinctured shield of arms at the top and a bronze relief portrait at the foot.

From this point it is suggested that the visitor explores the south and then the north aisles of this central part of the crypt, reaching the former by retracing his steps clockwise as far as bay three and passing to the right of Lord Napier's tomb. It seems appropriate to start with the south aisle (**T**) since it includes some monuments from old St Paul's as well as sculpture brought here from elsewhere in the cathedral. The non-monumental sculptures are the two fine urns or incense pots, dating from the time of Wren and carved by Cibber, and brought inside to preserve them from further deterioration. The monuments, clockwise, are:

159. William Hewit, d. 1599, a typical-looking City merchant in his fur-lined gown. Only the upper part of the effigy and the tomb-slab are preserved.

160. Two seated figures, presumably husband and wife; late sixteenth-century. This and the Hewit effigy are both still, poignantly, fire-blackened: a vivid reminder of the Fire of London (1666).

161. Admiral Sir Pulteney Malcolm, d. 1838. Colossal standing marble figure, with telescope, by Edward Hodges Baily RA 1842.

162. Lord Rodney, 1718–1792, Vice Admiral of England. It is a substantial composition by John Charles Felix Rossi RA (dated 1815), in which the admiral is shown as it were on deck flanked by figures (respectfully at a lower level) of Fame (seated, recording his exploits) and Victory. It was originally in the north transept, and deserves a more spacious and prominent setting. Paid for by Parliament (£6,000).

163. Tomb-chest on which are mounted five pre-Fire shields and (unconnected with them) part of a ledger of the bishop of Chester who died in 1661.

164. Pre-Fire effigies, the lower parts missing, of Thomas (d. 1594) and Anna (d. 1592) Heneage. Also fire-blackened.

165. Dean Henry Milman, 1791–1868. Priest, poet, historian and theologian and a famous nineteenth-century Dean of St Paul's. He was given a splendid full-length effigy, of impressive quality, by Francis John Williamson (1876); it stands on a Wren-style tomb-chest. Removed from the south choir aisle, and deserving of a more prominent position.

166. General William Napier, 1785–1860. Historian of the Peninsular War. Colossal marble statue by E H Baily RA but not, alas, of the quality of 161 or 162.

167. General Sir Charles Napier, 1782–1853. Brother of William, the sculpture is by George Gamon Adams.

From this point the order becomes more complicated. The cross-aisle (**U**) will be dealt with next, beginning with the west side:

168. Pilot Officer W M L Fiske, an American airman who fought in the Battle of Britain, d. 18

August 1940. Freestone Neo-Classical tablet in the style of c. 1770, and very refined. By Sir Albert Richardson, PRA.

169. William Huggins, 1824–1910. Neo-Classical tablet in white marble with relief portrait of the astronomer enclosed by a laurel wreath. A smaller roundel with relief portrait of his wife below. By Henry Pegram RA, whose work is well represented in St Paul's.

170. Baroque-style marble tablet to members of the Metropolitan Corps of the St John's Ambulance Brigade who died in the South African War of 1899–1902.

171. Edward Vansittart Neale, 1810–1892. An important figure in the history of the Trade Union movement. An attractive monument, by Sir George Frampton RA, with wilful lettering eloquent of the 1890s and a relief portrait over which a figure of Fame blows her trumpet.

172. George Cruikshank, 1792–1878. A painter and etcher remembered for his vivid portrayal of London life in the mid-nineteenth century, and a campaigner for abstention from alcohol. Plain marble tablet with cramped lettering. More striking is the large ledger in the floor nearby, with telling use of black, red and white marble. By John Adams-Acton.

173. Viscount Camrose, 1879–1954. A distinguished Neo-Classical design, perhaps by Lord Mottistone. Oval in shape, white marble with pinkish-brown border.

174. W E Henley, 1849–1903, poet. A freestone frame and console bracket in the style of Wren furnishes the setting for a fine portrait head by Auguste Rodin.

Then cross over to the north side of the cross-aisle:

175. Sir Charles Pritchard, 1836–1903. Served in India, as civil servant and Minister of the Indian Empire. Freestone tablet, with interesting lettering and shield of arms.

176. Sir George Grey, 1812–98. Governor and Premier of New Zealand. Red marble wall tablet in Renaissance style. A bracket supports a portrait bust by Edward Onslow Ford RA, 1901. Close by in the floor one of the half dozen or so really fine brass ledgers in the crypt, which has also a portrait in relief and good raised lettering.

177. W M Hughes, CH, 1864–1952. Prime Minister of Australia. Refined freestone tablet with inset bronze relief head showing a distinctive profile.

178. William Bede Dalley, 1831–88. Australian statesman and patriot. A carefully considered monument both in design and materials.

179. Richard Seddon, 1845–1906. Prime Minister of New Zealand. A fine monument, though less for the white marble portrait bust in high relief than for the exuberant bronze frame in idiosyncratic *fin-de-siècle* Baroque style, all by Sir George Frampton RA, 1909. The frame is crowned by wreaths and ribbons, and the inscription panel flanked by female figures of Administration and Justice.

180. Sir Bartle Frere, 1815–84. A remarkable composition of wall monument and ledger which, together with the surrounding area of floor, encompasses a whole

bay. The ledger has attractive borders and a central cross using red marble against white. The paving alternates black marble squares with groups of mottled pink squares, and the outer border of black marble recites Bartle Frere's family ramifications. The wall monument is Jacobean in style, with volutes and strapwork and a well-carved achievement of arms. The inscription tells of his numerous honours and exploits in India, South Africa and England.

Returning east along the north side of the Nelson tomb-chamber (**V**) there are two more monuments blackened in the Great Fire of 1666.

181. William Cokain, d. 1626. Freestone effigy showing him in ruff and rich clothes, hands and feet missing.

182. Sir Nicholas Bacon, 1509–79, Queen Elizabeth I's Lord Keeper of the Great Seal, father of Lord Chancellor Francis Bacon. Freestone effigy, the lower half of which is missing.

Also in the north aisle:

183. Sir Philip Sidney, 1554–86. Romantic figure at the court of Queen Elizabeth I, famous for his poetry as well as for his role as diplomat and soldier. One of the most distinctive and enjoyable recent arrivals in St Paul's, by David Kindersley and Lida Lopes Cardozo (1985). Elegantly-shaped tablet of Cumbrian slate, the lettering is itself a particular pleasure; above it an oval medallion with Palombino marble portrait head in relief, sensitive and alert.

In this aisle the visitor would be well advised to pause and examine the well-displayed memorabilia associated with Wren and the cathedral, which are described on p. 118, and also visit the Treasury.

In the Treasury (W), in a recess on the west side:

184. Charles Oman, 1901–82. By David Kindersley. Oval Welsh slate tablet with lettering leafed with platignum to a much-loved figure who was Keeper of Metalwork at the Victoria and Albert Museum and author of the standard book on *Anglican Church Plate*, and who inspired the Worshipful Company of Goldsmiths to found cathedral treasuries where gold and silver vessels and other works of art could be displayed, shared and enjoyed.

To continue the tour of the monuments, we retrace our steps westwards, pass beyond the cross aisle to the south aisle of the nave of the crypt (**X**), and explore the remainder of the monuments again in a clockwise direction.

185. Charles Reade, 1814–84. Dramatist and journalist. White marble tablet on grey, incorporating a portrait relief in oval frame. Signed by G M Curtice.

186. Sir Walter Besant, 1836–1901. Best remembered now not so much as a novelist but as a historian of London and founder of the Society of Authors. Most enjoyable monument, showing Besant with his *pince-nez* framed by jolly swags and ribbons. Good lettering. All in bronze, and readily recognisable as the work of Sir George Frampton, RA.

187. George M Smith, 1824–1901. Editor of the *Dictionary of National Biography*. Streaky pink marble on mottled green. Alabaster inscription tablet with the excellent lettering so charac-

teristic of the turn of the century, framed in mosaic.

188. Sir William Alexander Smith, 1854–1914. Founder of the Boys' Brigade (1883). Tall narrow tablet in Nabresina with portrait bust in low relief and excellent coloured lettering. By David Kindersley.

189. Prebendary Wilson Carlile, CH, 1847–1942. Founder of the Church Army. Pleasing Classical-inspired tablet, good lettering, portrait relief in a wreath. Freestone.

Beyond the Great Model, and much further to the west (**Y**) in a shallow niche:

190. Earl St Vincent, d. 1823, who took his title from the famous victory over the Spanish fleet at Cape St Vincent in 1797. Colossal standing figure by E H Baily RA, 1826. Originally in the north transept, and paid for by Parliament (£2,000).

191. James Watt, 1736–1819, improver of the steam engine and therefore a founding father of the English 'industrial revolution'. Thoughtful, seated figure of the philosopher-inventor, by Sir Francis Chantrey RA. Brought here from the Transport Museum at Clapham, to which it had been taken from Westminster Abbey. The convex inscription panel has a fine turn in phraseology, a quality in which the memorial inscriptions of St Paul's are not conspicuously rich, perhaps being self-conscious of their position.

192. Sir William Ponsonby, who died at Waterloo on 18 June 1815. Erected by Parliament (£3,150) and originally in the north transept. One cannot help but enjoy the swagger of these monuments

of the Napoleonic wars. This one shows the dying hero, naked but for a little drapery, leaning against his stricken horse while a winged figure of Fame holds out to him a victor's wreath, much as angels in Baroque paintings of martyrdom hold out the martyr's palm-frond. Designed by William Theed RA and carved by E H Baily RA.

193. Mountstuart Elphinstone, 1779–1859. Wrote a history of India. Colossal marble figure by Matthew Noble, 1863, but in the manner of half a century earlier. Moved here from the north transept.

Crossing to the north aisle (Z)
194. Viscount Duncan, d. 1804. A naval hero, shown as a tall standing figure in his peer's robes with a sword. By Sir Richard Westmacott RA. The head seems of better quality than the rest. Erected by Parliament (£2,100) and originally in the north transept.

195. Captain James Mosse and Captain Edward Riou, who both died in Nelson's sea battle at Copenhagen in 1801. The inscription is well worth reading, especially for the tale of heroism on the part of Captain Riou after an earlier ship of his had struck an 'Island of Ice'. As a design this is one of the most enjoyable and impressive of its period (by John Charles Felix Rossi RA, 1805): a noble Neo-Classical sarcophagus, ornamented with lions' heads, rests on a convex plinth. Against this two giant winged figures, one female and one male, hold admirably well-characterized portrait medallions of Mosse and Riou. Erected by Parliament (£4,200) and originally in the north transept.

196. Not a memorial, but worthy of notice, is a freestone tablet giving the names of Head Virgers and Clerks of the Works of St Paul's Cathedral from 1663 onwards.

197. Henry Hallam, 1777–1859. Constitutional historian. Tall standing figure by William Theed RA, 1862, and seemingly forming a pair with that to Elphinstone (No 193).

198. In a recess, the names and dates of some of those (there must have been countless more) who were buried in old St Paul's. Amongst these 'famous dead' are the two Saxon kings, Sebba and Ethelred; John of Gaunt, Duke of Lancaster; Thomas Linacre, the founder of the Royal College of Physicians; and Sir Anthony Van Dyck, painter at the court of Charles I. Although there is not much 'design', the lettering is good.

199. Opposite Penrose's pulpit is a ledger, of interest in that it is to James Lamon, d. 1868, a virger, and his wife Ann, d. 1862. Another virger, John Hicks, d. 1853, lies buried beneath a ledger on the south side, east of Earl St Vincent's memorial.

200. Sir George Williams, 1821–1905. Founder of the YMCA. Another beautiful piece of sculpture by Sir George Frampton RA (1908), this time all in marble. Against a tall back-panel, with a sun-burst like an eighteenth-century reredos, a sympathetic portrait bust of Sir George. The plinth which supports it is flanked by seated female figures holding curious orbs. Close by, but a distinctive work of art in its own right, is Sir George Williams' magnificent brass ledger.

201. Lord Holford, 1907–75. The architect who was consultant for the rebuilding of the City of London after the Second World War, responsible for the concept of Paternoster Square. *Circumspice.* In layout and lettering this small but distinguished tablet in dark grey slate is a paradigm of what a good but modest memorial should be like. By Richard Kindersley.

202. Duff Cooper, Viscount Norwich, 1890–1954. Statesman and writer. Modest tablet in dark grey slate. Terse, but good, lettering.

203. Lord Thomson of Fleet, 1894–1976. Newspaper magnate. Black slate tablet with gold lettering, interesting inscription. By David Kindersley.

204. George Swan Nottage, d. 1885. He died in office, in the Mansion House, when Lord Mayor of London. Like the adjoining memorial to Sir Bartle Frere, this is an unusual case of a wall monument and a ledger with its surround forming a single artistic design. The wall monument is in Baroque style, perhaps to distinguish it from Frere's, and is conspicious for the careful and successful choice of different coloured marbles. In the centre is a roundel with portrait in relief framed by the mayoral chain and other symbols of office. The brass, inscribed with the maker's name (Hart, Son, Peard and Co) incorporates a portrait of him in full mayoral costume. Altogether, a very fine ensemble.

THE CATHEDRAL CHURCH

The ordering and numbering of the monuments assumes that the visitor will have begun the tour of the monuments with those in the crypt. For those with an inexhaustible appetite for monuments the tour of the main floor level of the cathedral entails starting again at the north-west entrance. In the north-west vestibule is the entrance to the *Chapel of All Souls* (also known as the *Kitchener Memorial Chapel*) under the north-west tower. This door is usually locked (notice the superb early eighteenth-century decoration of the key-hole), and access is by application to the virgers.

205. Chapel of All Souls
This chapel is an intense, compelling space in which almost everything is of stone, marble or iron. The architecture is Wren's: a square room with canted corners which support the broad ribs of the vault. The ribs are ornamented with recessed panels, alternately rectangular and square, and support an octagonally framed centrepiece carved with oak leaves and acorns. The furnishings and sculpture are an ensemble of the 1920s, and they comprise the fine stone altar with its frieze of *putti*, and integral with it the reredos with a noble inscription in gilt lettering and above it Sir William Reid Dick's KCVO, RA moving *Pietà*. On the west wall is an inscription tablet recording the creation of the chapel as a memorial to Field Marshal Earl Kitchener (d. 1916, when the ship in which he was sailing, HMS *Hampshire*, sank off the coast of Orkney) and to all those who fell in the World War of 1914–18. Flanking it are figures of the military saints, Michael and George, and then centrally placed before them is the superb white marble effigy of Kitchener. A special pleasure of this chapel is the high quality of the lettering, and another is the metal-work including the gates, the aumbry grilles in the north wall, and the standard candlesticks by William Bainbridge Reynolds. The altar cross and candlesticks are of silver and crystal.

Bay one of the north aisle
206. Lord Leighton, 1830–96. Both a painter and a sculptor, one of his best-known works is *Physical Energy* in Kensington Palace Gardens. Also in Kensington is his own remarkable house, which is now open as the Lord Leighton's House Museum. He lies buried in the crypt (No 41) under a brass ledger designed by the architect Richard Norman Shaw RA, but here his monument occupies a prominent place in the cathedral and is one of the outstanding masterpieces of Sir Thomas Brock KCB, RA (who had the bronze parts cast in Brussels). Leighton's effigy, dressed as President of the Royal Academy, lies on a Renaissance-style sarcophagus; all this is of bronze, and rests on a plinth of different coloured marbles. On either side are allegorical figures representing painting and sculpture, the latter holding in her hand a miniature of Leighton's *Sluggard*.

The Chapel of All Souls—a remarkable memorial ensemble of the 1920s (no. 205).

207. Archbishop Frederick Temple, 1821–1902. He had been Bishop of London for eleven years, and hence a memorial to him here as well as in Canterbury cathedral. Large bronze plaque, on which is the kneeling figure of the Archbishop in high relief. By Frederick Pomeroy RA, 1905.

208. A memorial to those members of the Cavalry Division who died in the war with Russia 1854–56. Tripartite marble memorial filling curved panel below window, with reliefs left and right showing cavalrymen on horseback. Dull.

Between bays one and two
209. Field Marshal Lord Slim, 1891–1970. Tablet in Nabresina marble with good lettering painted red or gilded.

Bay two
210. Major General Charles George Gordon, 1833–85. He died heroically, as the inscription records. Not so princely a monument as Leighton's, but still fine, his bronze effigy by Sir Edgar Boehm Bart., RA lies on a black marble sarcophagus, which is supported on cast bronze claw feet. On the far side is a charming relief showing Gordon visiting a school room in Khartoum.

211. Marble relief panel illustrating a text from II Samuel 'Is not this the blood of the men that went in jeopardy of their lives?' This, which is by James Forsyth (1883), and the brass plaque beneath are in memory of members of the Royal Fusiliers who died in the Afghan campaign of 1879–80.

212. Sir Herbert Stewart,

LEFT: Detail of Sir William Reid Dick's Pietà in the Chapel of All Souls (no. 205).
RIGHT: The Sluggard, miniature bronze figure on Sir Thomas Brock's memorial to
Lord Leighton (no. 206).

1843–85. As a dashing soldier in early middle age he led the Desert Column in the Nile Expedition to relieve Khartoum, and died in battle. The long curved relief panel has a central portrait medallion and over it what seems to be his funeral procession in the desert, with camels. By Sir Edgar Boehm Bart., RA.

213. Sir Arthur Wellesley Torrens, d. 1855 of wounds received at Inkermann in the Crimea. Spirited marble relief panel, showing Torrens on horseback in the thick of the battle.

214. Arthur Wellesley, first Duke of Wellington, Field Marshal, 1769–1852. In the crypt Wellington's body lies in the huge red porphyry sarcophagus which is now the focal point for the commemoration of the great military commanders of the Second World War. Here his monument occupies the central bay of the north nave arcade and is one of the most celebrated English works of art of the nineteenth century. Its concept, and much of its execution, was the work of Alfred Stevens—a great, if unstable, genius. The genesis of it, and the trials and tribulations of its accomplishment, are fully described in a book called *The Wellington Monument* by John Physick (London, 1970). The main part of the monument was carried out between 1858 and 1878, and the equestrian sculpture of the Duke of Wellington on top was realized by John Tweed between 1899 and 1912. Essentially, it is a triumphal arch raised above a substantial base. Within the arch lies the effigy of the Duke on a mighty sarcophagus, all in

bronze. The plinth supporting the sarcophagus is sculpted with military trophies. Above the arch is an attic storey, with the motif of the Order of the Garter; either side are pairs of figures representing *Valour and Cowardice* (facing west) and *Truth and Falsehood* (facing east). These figures show the influence of Michelangelo very strongly and, indeed, the whole stupendous performance evokes the commemoration of a Renaissance military hero and prince.

Between bays two and three
215. Field Marshal Earl Roberts, VC KG KP 1832–1914. A striking dignified white marble bust in an oval niche forming part of a larger setting in white, black, and richly veined marbles and bronze.

216. Opposite is a well-lettered tablet within a frame of black Belgian marble to commemorate the faithful volunteer service in the Indian Army from 1747 to 1947. By such memorials is St Paul's knitted into the fabric of English history, and linked with both the former Empire and the present high ideals of the Commonweath of Nations. Made by John Skelton in 1970. Also by him is the inscription cut into the plinth below, and a small bronze and marble tablet set into the floor commemorating the Women's Auxiliary Corps India 1942–4.

Bay three
217. The brass plaques on either side record the sad circumstances behind the loss of HMS *Captain* off Cape Finisterre in 1870, and the names of all those who drowned. It seems odd to quote a

court verdict on a memorial, but adds greatly to the interest of it.

218. The centrepiece of the bay, which intrudes cruelly on the architecture, is Baron Marochetti's monument to two successive Lords Melbourne: William, d. 1848, who was Queen Victoria's first Prime Minister; and Frederick, d. 1853, who was his brother. It takes the form of a full-scale representation of the entrance portal to a mausoleum or burial vault, in black marble and bronze, flanked by tall dreamy figures of angels in white marble. One holds a sword, the other a trumpet.

219. In the bay below the northwest pier of the dome are four alabaster plaques recording the names and dates of Deans of St Paul's since 1066.

220. Sir Joshua Reynolds, 1723–92, one of England's (or the world's) finest portrait painters. Tall standing figure in white marble, on a plinth. His left hand rests on a pedestal, which has a portrait medallion showing a certain 'M. Angelo'. His right hand clutches a volume to his breast, no doubt representing a handsomely-bound edition of his celebrated *Discourses on Art*, for Reynolds was a notable theorist as well as painter and President of the Royal Academy. He looks rather donnish, and anxious. The sculpture is by John Flaxman RA, one of the outstanding sculptors of the English Neo-Classical period.

North transept, west aisle
221. Charles Robert Cockerell RA, 1788–1863. A major Neo-Classical architect, and an auth-

OPPOSITE: Dreamily beautiful figure of an angel, detail of Baron Marochetti's Melbourne memorial (no. 218).

ority on Classical antiquities. He shared in the discovery of important Classical Greek sculptures, and was one of the first to observe the entasis on Greek columns. He was also responsible for a famous drawing entitled *A Tribute to the Memory of Sir Christopher Wren* (1838), showing all Wren's buildings assembled as a single group and during his time as Surveyor of the Fabric of St Paul's the ball and cross on the dome were replaced (1821–2). His wall monument shows an Ionic column, of the kind he was fond of using, and on it is suspended a portrait medallion. Below this, winged angels kneel back to back in fervent prayer. Beautifully lettered inscription panel. Perhaps designed by F C Penrose, Cockerell's successor as Surveyor. Both lie buried in the crypt below.

222. Major General Daniel Hoghton, who 'fell gloriously' at the Battle of Albuera, 1811. High up, and it is interesting to see how it and those in similar positions ingeniously use the space and perspective available to them. Here, Hoghton is sprawled out to fill the length of the panel, but sits up taking a keen interest in the progress of the battle. The winged figure of Fame courteously lifts a standard, so that he can see a little better, and holds the victor's laurel wreath in readiness. By Sir Francis Chantrey RA.

223. Lieutenant Colonel Sir William Myers, Hoghton's comrade-in-arms at Albuera, is commemorated opposite. Over the rather verbose inscription tablet is a portrait bust on a plinth. A rather lascivious-looking fellow is occupied in giving Britannia a leg-up for a better look. By Joseph Kendrick (d. 1832).

224. A marble relief panel showing *Christ the Consoler*. Together with the brass plaque below it is a memorial to those members of the 57th West Middlesex Regiment who died in the Crimean War or in New Zealand. By James Forsyth (1877), following the same pattern as No 211.

225. Lieutenant General Sir Thomas Picton, who died at Waterloo (Wellington's decisive victory) in 1815. A large marble group, in which a portrait bust of Picton stands on a tall plinth in front of and to the side of which are allegorical figures of immortality, military victory and victory accompanied by a lion. By Sebastian Gahagan (fl. 1800–35), a Dublin-born sculptor who worked for Nollekens and whose most important independent work this is.

226. A marble relief commemorating men of the 77th East Middlesex Regiment who died in the Crimean War. Soldiers are shown contemplating the mass graves of their fallen comrades while, in the midst, hovers a consoling angel whose sombre mood seems to match theirs. By Matthew Noble (d. 1876), one of three works by him in St Paul's.

North transept, central bay
227. Major General Andrew Hay, d. 1814 at Bayonne in France. Life-size marble group, raised off the floor, showing Hay at the moment of his death supported by a naked figure who looks curiously like a Greek god while the soldier on the left, though pensive, appears indifferent to what is going on. Commissioned by the House of Commons in 1814 from Humphrey Hopper (b. 1767), but not a major success.

LEFT: *Memorial to C R Cockerell (no. 221).*
RIGHT: *Memorial to Major General Thomas Dundas (no. 229), which quotes Parliament's resolution to erect a memorial to him.*

228. Another Neo-Classical monument, this time to *two* Major Generals, Arthur Gore and John Byne Skerrett, who died at Bergen-op-Zoom, 1814. Entirely allegorical, showing the seated Britannia being comforted by Immortality. One of four works in St Paul's by Sir Francis Chantrey RA, an immensely successful sculptor whose fortune established the Chantrey Bequest at the Royal Academy.

229. Major General Thomas Dundas, d. 1794. Interesting historically because it quotes the Parliamentary resolution which requested King George III to direct that a monument should be erected to Dundas in St Paul's, and artistically in that it is a major work by the sculptor John Bacon,

junior, dating from 1805. A handsome portrait bust stands on a large pedestal on which is a relief sculpture of great beauty. A proud Britannia holds a laurel wreath over Dundas's head, and accompanying her are figures emblematic of peace and plenty.

230. Above it is a marble memorial in high relief to Major General J R Mackenzie and Brigadier General E Langwerth, d. 1809, a complex allegorical group by Charles Manning (d. 1812), a member of a prolific family of sculptors and himself responsible in St Paul's for the monument to Captain George Hardinge (1808).

231. Opposite Dundas's is the large marble group commemorating the young naval hero Captain

Robert Faulkner, who died in battle in 1795. Neo-Classical sentiment allowed the sculptor to portray the lightly-clad Faulkner as dying in the arms of King Neptune while a winged Victory proffers the laurel wreath. By John Charles Felix Rossi dating from 1805, and one of five monuments by him in St Paul's.

North transept, east aisle
232. Major General Bernard Bowes, who died in the assault on Salamanca in 1812. The scene is depicted in a memorable panel of relief sculpture. By Sir Francis Chantrey, RA.

233. Sir Arthur Sullivan (d. 1900), the composer. Impressive bronze plaque, showing *Orpheus with his lyre* and below a portrait medallion held by *putti*.

234. Major General John Le Marchant (d. 1812). Large marble group in high relief showing a sarcophagus with allegorical figures. It is signed by James Smith (d. 1815) but, apparently, though designed by him it was carved after his death by John Charles Felix Rossi RA who also sent his widow a present of £200.

235. Sir John Stainer, composer of church music and organist of St Paul's from 1872 to 1888. Tall thin marble tablet carved in low relief with portrait medallion below and a vision of the seated Christ adored by angels above. By Henry Pegram RA, 1903.

North-east corner of the crossing
236. Samuel Johnson (i.e. 'Dr Johnson'). The great lexicographer is shown leaning on a column, his left leg brought strongly forward. By John Bacon RA the elder in 1795.

South-east corner of the crossing
237. John Howard. An impressive figure sculpture, again by John Bacon RA, in which the reformer of prisons is shown stepping boldly forward, a key in his right hand and his 'Plan for the improvement of prisons' in his left. The long inscription on the right-hand side of the plinth is well worth reading, and especially enjoyable is the relief on the front.

South transept, east aisle
238. Captain Robert Scott and his companions who died on the return journey from the South Pole in 1912. Bronze tablet superficially in the Baroque manner but unmistakably of the early twentieth century. By S Nicholson Babb.

239. Over the entrance to the crypt is the memorial to Major General Robert Ross, who d. 1814 whilst attacking the city of Baltimore (he had already successfully attacked the city of Washington). An elaborate group in high relief in which Britannia mourns her loss, Victory holds half a laurel wreath over the hero's portrait bust and a naked male figure presumably personifies military valour. By Josephus Kendrick (1791–1832, son of Joseph Kendrick), 1821.

240. Major General Sir John Jones, d. 1843. Tall standing figure of a distinguished soldier by William Behnes. Behnes was a prolific sculptor, whose statue of Dr Babington (1837) is also in St Paul's.

241. Sir Henry Lawrence, who d. in the defence of Lucknow 1857. Tall standing figure and not inspiring. More enjoyable is the small relief showing him with his wife and three children. By J G Lough (d. 1876) in 1862.

242. Colonel Henry Cadogan, who d. 1813 at Vittoria. A really fine relief sculpture, and a pendant to No 228 which, like this one, is by Chantrey.

South transept, east bay

243. Admiral Earl Howe, d. 1799. A staggering composition in white marble, which fills the whole space beneath the window and is one of John Flaxman's masterpieces. Lord Howe is shown standing, his right arm balanced on his telescope which rests upon the plinth on which sits Britannia. To the right crouches the British lion, while to the left two female figures trace an inscription recording two of his greatest victories. Flaxman RA did this in 1803, and his still finer monument to Nelson nearby in 1809.

244. Admiral Lord Collingwood, d. 1810, who commanded a division in the great naval battle at Trafalgar in 1805. In many respects one of the most striking and memorable monuments in the cathedral. It is by Richard Westmacott RA (d. 1856) in 1813, and is superbly carved. It shows the recumbent figure of Collingwood in a funeral barge, as befits a naval hero, protected by an angel; to the right is a figure based on a classical river god. The five tiny *putti* inhabiting the scrollwork on the sides of the barge are particularly deliciously carved.

245. J M W Turner, RA, d. 1851, one of the most celebrated British painters of the nineteenth-century who bequeathed a large collection of his own work to the nation. The standing figure sculpture is by Patrick MacDowell RA (d. 1810). The pose is lively, the head good.

246. General Lord Heathfield who, as Governor, defended Gibraltar in 1782 and d. 1790. Standing figure, his military costume well shown but the head lacking conviction. By John Charles Felix Rossi RA, 1825.

South transept, centre bay

247. Double monument with two standing figures to Major General Sir Edward Pakenham and Major General Samuel Gibbs who d. 1815 in an attack before New Orleans. The shorter rests an arm on the shoulder of the taller and the result is both convincing and touching. Like so many of the monuments in St Paul's this one would richly repay cleaning and conservation. By Sir Richard Westmacott RA, 1823.

248. Major General Robert Gillespie who d. 1814 at Kalunga, Nepal. Tall standing figure, competent rather than inspired. Unsigned.

249. Vice-Admiral Viscount Nelson, the outstanding naval hero of the Napoleonic wars, who died in the battle of Trafalgar, 1805. A major work by John Flaxman RA, 1808–18. The hero stands, in his peer's robes, with his left hand resting on an anchor. The drum-like plinth has a wonderful frieze of sea-gods. To the right of the plinth crouches the British lion (how many lions are there, one wonders, in St Paul's? Wellington's tomb alone has twelve), while to the left Britannia commends the example of Nelson's heroism to two schoolboys.

250. Captain George Hardinge, a young naval officer who died near Ceylon in 1808. Sculpture in high relief by Charles Manning, in which an Indian figure sits pensively by the fallen hero's sarcophagus while a winged Victory mourns disconsolately.

MONUMENTS IN THE CATHEDRAL CHURCH

251. Marquess Cornwallis, a notable Governor of Bengal, who died 1805. As a composition this is memorable, and also for the exotic Indian figure on the left. Cornwallis himself stands on a tall fluted plinth, dressed as a Knight of the Garter. Two other Indian figures are shown to the right. By John Charles Felix Rossi RA, 1811.

252. Captain R Willett Miller, by John Flaxman RA (1801). Although placed high up over the Cornwallis monument this is a fine relief sculpture in which Britannia (accompanied by the British lion) and Victory hang a plaque on a palm tree recording Miller's part in the battles off Cape St Vincent and the Nile.

South transept, between centre and west bays

253. Memorial to the 4,300 citizens of Australia, Canada, Ceylon, New Zealand and South Africa who fought for Britain and d. in the South African War of 1899–1902. It takes the form of a bronze sculpture of Christ being released from the cross by a winged female figure whose molten Baroque draperies pour down behind and in front of the cross. This stands on a bracket, below which is the inscription tablet. It is a remarkable work of art, which deserves to be better known, and it is by Princess Louise, Duchess of Argyll (1904), sculptress daughter of Queen Victoria.

254. Captain Sir William Hoste. Tall standing figure by Thomas Campbell (d. 1858), 1833.

South transept, west bay
255. Tablet recording a vanished

window nearby which had been installed to commemorate Queen Victoria's solemn visit in 1872 to give thanks for the recovery of the Prince of Wales from a dangerous illness. The tablet is itself an agreeable combination of marble, alabaster and mosaic work; and it reminds us that, until they were destroyed in the Second World War, nineteenth-century stained glass windows of considerable artistic interest gave the interior of the cathedral a very different appearance from that which we now enjoy.

256. Lt General Sir John Moore, d. 1809. Another British hero of the Napoleonic era, killed at Corunna in northern Spain. An important work by John Bacon the younger (1815) in which the hero is portrayed being lowered into a sarcophagus by Victory and a handsome naked female figure. A *putto* holding a furled standard with the victor's laurel wreath gives height and drama to the composition.

257. Sir Astley Paston Cooper, d. 1842. Surgeon to Guy's Hospital and to three successive sovereigns. A notable innovator, he is shown in an academic gown, his left hand resting upon a book. As other memorials in the vicinity show, it is difficult to make this kind of solo standing figure an artistic success; and yet the head is impressive enough. By Edward Hodges Baily, RA.

258. Lieutenant General Sir Ralph Abercromby, who d. 1801 whilst successfully landing his troops on Egyptian soil in the war against Napoleon. A large and powerful sculptural group by Richard

OPPOSITE: The South African War Memorial, by HRH Princess Louise, Duchess of Argyll (no. 253).

Westmacott RA, in which Sir Ralph expires on horseback, supported by an aide. The relationship between the two principal figures is well managed, and yet there is a certain bathos about the work as a whole which is not helped by the strong light from the window behind. The main group is flanked by sphinxes, which makes a nice change from lions.

259. Admiral Lord Lyons, d. 1858, by Matthew Noble. Tall standing figure in white marble, by a sculptor who was more than competent.

260. Major General Sir Isaac Brock, d. 1812 at Queenstown, Canada. All the relief sculptures placed high up in the transepts are worth looking at, and this one is no exception. The idealized hero expires in the arms of a comrade-in-arms, while an American Indian in a splendid headdress looks on with polite sympathy rather than hostility. By Richard Westmacott, RA.

261. William Babington, d. 1833. Tall standing figure of a notable physician, shown (like Astley Cooper) in academic dress, but in a more interesting and sympathetic pose. By William Behnes, 1837.

262. Sir William Jones, d. 1794, commemorated by the East India Company for his services as a judge in Bengal. This is the last to be encountered of the four fine figure sculptures in the corners below the dome; their installation opened the floodgates to a profusion of monuments in St Paul's which had previously been staved off. This one is also by John Bacon the elder RA (1799) and, like the other three, he is shown in classical

dress. There is a lively turn of the head, a suppleness to the body, and much fine detail (e.g. on the strap across his torso, on the desk supporting his books, and on the plinth below depicting Indian deities) so that this is one of the more enjoyable figure sculptures in St Paul's.

263. In the bay below the southwest pier of the dome are alabaster tablets to the bishops of London from Restitutus (314) and Mellitus (604) to the present bishop of the diocese, Dr Graham Leonard (1981).

South nave aisle, first bay from the east

264. Captain Granville Gower Loch, d. 1853, near Donabew on the river Irrawaddy in Burma. A curved relief plaque, also unsigned, but most enjoyable. It depicts the youthful hero scaling impossible odds against the natives, and conjures up the world of *Tom Brown's Schooldays*.

265. Dominating the centre of the bay, and taking us back to the Napoleonic era again is the striking monument by Thomas Banks RA (1805, shortly before he died) to Captain George Westcott who was killed in the sea battle off Aboukir in 1798. It consists of two elements: the hero dying on the arm of Victory, on a large oval-shaped plinth; and, more enjoyably, the three reliefs on the plinth showing the battle at its height, a river god representing the Nile and surrounded by *putti* one of whom is sporting on an alligator, and a ship at anchor with a pyramid close by. The river god reflects a Classical Roman prototype.

266. Behind Banks's *Westcott* is a

large curved panel carved by W Calder Marshall RA (1863). It appears to depict the *Blessed in Paradise*.

267. Captain Edmund Lyons (son of Admiral Lord Lyons, No 259) who died in 1855 on board HMS *Miranda* whilst firing on the fortifications of Sevastapol in the Crimea. The incident is represented in a lively manner on a curved white marble tablet, above a portrait relief of the young naval hero. It shows that HMS *Miranda* combined both sails and steam.

South nave aisle, second bay
268. Dominating this bay is the large monument to Dr Thomas Middleton, d. 1822, by J G Lough (1832). Middleton was the first Anglican bishop in India, consecrated Bishop of Calcutta in 1814, and is depicted in the immense lawn sleeves of his day confirming two Indian children with dramatic gesture.

269 and 270. On either side are curved panels depicting texts from the book of *Job* and gospel of *Matthew* by W Calder Marshall (d. 1894). They seem to have originally formed a group with the large central panel in bay one. Although Marshall was a Royal Academician, it cannot be said that these panels are inspired.

South nave aisle, third bay
271. Richard Rundle Burges, d. 1797 in the naval engagement off Camperdowne. This noble sculptural group is earlier (1802) than the same artist's (Thomas Banks RA) monument to Westcott (No 265), which effectively forms a pendant to this one. Here the concept is established: on a large oval-shaped plinth stands the naked naval commander, as gla-

morous as a Greek god or a modern film-star, and a classically-draped Victory hands him a sword in a scabbard. A beautifully ornamented cannon stands between. The plinth is superbly carved with figures in high relief.

272, 273 and 274. In the three curved panels of this bay are set relief sculptures by Frederick Woodington ARA (d. 1893) who had been awarded the second premium in the competition for the *Wellington* monument. These three reliefs were originally in the Consistory Court (now the Chapel of St Michael and St George) nearby, and date from 1862: they illustrate, in a late Neo-Classical vein, texts from *Luke, Genesis* and *Psalm 140* and are artistically much more satisfying than those by W Calder Marshall in bays one and two.

South nave vestibule
275. A bronze relief tablet to members of the Coldstream Guards who died in the South African War of 1899–1902. Unlike its pedestrian opposite number this is a deeply-felt example of memorial art and is signed by Sir William Goscombe John RA, 1902.

276. A tablet with two Coldstream guardsmen carved in relief commemorating eight of their comrades who died in the battle of Inkermann in the Crimea (1854).

The South choir aisle
277. Bishop Charles Blomfield, d. 1857. By George Richmond 'Pictor' (i.e. painter), the father of Sir William Richmond who designed the mosaics in the eastern arm of the cathedral. White marble recumbent effigy on a tomb-chest. It is instructive to compare

LEFT: Hollar's engraving of Nicholas Stone's effigy of John Donne (no. 278). The only monument to survive the Great Fire of 1666 intact.
RIGHT: Detail.

the style of episcopal dress with that of Mandell Creighton opposite.

278. John Donne, Dean of St Paul's and one of our finest poets, d. 1631. This was the only monument to survive the Great Fire of 1666 intact, and it is a masterpiece by Nicholas Stone, one of the leading sculptors at the time of King Charles I. The figure of the poet-priest is shown in his burial shroud, with a folded top-knot, his face turned towards the spectator's right. It is a moving, haunting, image and justly one of the most celebrated works of art in the cathedral.

(West of Donne's monument are one or two small fragments of early sculpture with inscriptions recording them as having come from the Temple in Jerusalem.)

279. Bishop Mandell Creighton, d. 1901. By Sir Hamo Thornycroft RA (1905), and one of his best works. Full-size bronze figure of the bishop, benignly blessing; in his left hand he carries a crozier and, significantly for that date when it was a daring thing for Anglican bishops to do, he wears a cope. The sculpture stands on a base of green mottled marble, and has an architectural setting of bronze.

Chapter Seven

THE LIFE AND WORK OF ST PAUL'S

TODAY IN St Paul's cathedral the unceasing round of services, the *opus Dei* (literally, the 'work of God'), is performed faithfully and with due dignity of ceremonial; the music, in the hands of the Organist and Master of the Choristers, adds its lustre to the daily services and on special occasions; the building radiates a sense of welcome and friendliness, which owes a great deal to the professional zeal of the Head Virger and his colleagues on the one hand and to the volunteer enthusiasm and faithfulness of the Friends of St Paul's on the other. The building is superbly well cared for by a permanent workforce of skilled craftsmen under the immediate direction of a Clerk of Works, and with one of the leading conservation architects of our day as the Surveyor to the Fabric. The organization of the cathedral and its small army of staff is smoothly, efficiently, and unobtrusively managed by the Registrar and Receiver from the Chapter House on the north side of St Paul's. In every direction one looks, improvements have been made or are being made.

It would be understandable, therefore, to suppose that this had always been true. But a hundred and fifty years ago it was a very different story. In the 1830s the choir alone was used regularly for worship, while the transepts, dome area and nave presented empty echoing voids. Not only was the cathedral dirty and un-welcoming, but there was no form of heating. The Whig reformist and brilliant letter-writer Sydney Smith

St Paul's provides a superb setting for the liturgy, musical performances, and for special national occasions.

wrote, in November 1833, two years after his appointment as a canon: 'To go to St Paul's is certain death. The thermometer is several degrees below zero. My sentences are frozen as they come out of my mouth, and are thawed in the course of the summer, making strange noises and unexpected assertions in various parts of the church.'

At this period the services seem to have been well attended. In 1839 Sydney Smith claimed that there were 'very often' 150 people at the afternoon service on weekdays, and that on Sundays the choir was 'full to suffocation'. Mattins and Evensong were the staple forms of services, Holy Communion being celebrated after Mattins on Sundays if a sufficient number of people remained behind for it.

Slightly later than this Dr Temple, later Archbishop of Canterbury, attended St Paul's one Sunday morning, as a pious young man, intending to remain for the service of Holy Communion. When the earlier part of the service was over, a virger came across to him and said: 'I hope, sir, you are not intending to remain for the sacrament as this will give the Minor Canon the trouble of celebrating, which otherwise he will not do'. Not surprisingly the young Temple walked out of the cathedral. On another occasion, the energetic bishop Charles Blomfield (1786–1857), who built and consecrated many new churches in the Diocese of London during his busy episcopate, is said to have remarked to a lawyer friend whom he met one day on Ludgate Hill: 'I look at that great Cathedral and think of its large revenues and great responsibilities, and ask myself what good is it doing to this great city, and I feel compelled to answer, not to any single soul in it'.

In the early nineteenth century music and preaching were the principal embellishments of the life and worship of the cathedral. From 1796 to 1838 the Organist of St Paul's was Thomas Attwood, who had studied with Mozart in Vienna. He had at his disposal a choir of eight boys, and six professional men singers who were called vicars choral. The standard of singing, while Attwood was at the height of his powers, was high. Afterwards, it declined somewhat as an anecdote of the 1840s indicates: once, when the Hallelujah Chorus from Handel's *Messiah* was to be sung as an anthem, it turned out that there were no men singers other than a single bass and a single tenor. A message was sent up to the organ loft and the organist, by this time Sir John Goss, replied 'Do your best, and I will do the rest with the organ'.

On Holy Days and festivals sermons were preached by one of the four residentiary canons, or by a deputy, or by one of the prebendaries. On ordinary Sundays a preacher was nominated by the bishop. The residentiary canons all had other appointments in those days (for example, Dean Copleston was also Bishop of Llandaff from 1827 to 1849, and Sydney Smith continued to be the parish priest of Combe Florey in Somerset) but they were expected to observe their months of being in residence punctiliously, each taking three out of the twelve months of the year.

On the accession of Queen Victoria in 1837 Sydney Smith preached a sermon in St Paul's in which he exhorted her 'to worship God by loving peace'; and although he expressed the hope that she herself would reverence the Church of England, by frequenting its worship and by regulating her faith according to its precepts, he regarded this as fully compatible with acknowledgment of the right of others to worship according to freedom of conscience.

Even while the cathedral was still being built an admission fee was first introduced at St Paul's, in 1709. Known as stairs-foot money, the proceeds were applied to relieving the wants of those men who were injured during the progress of the works. The architect George Godwin, who published *A History and Description of St Paul's Cathedral* in 1837, gives the admission charges which then prevailed as follows: 'To view the monuments and body of the church, 2d. The whispering gallery, the outside galleries, the library, the model room, the geometrical staircase, and the great bell, 1s.6d. The clock, 2d. The ball and cross, 2s, and the crypt, 1s, making in the whole, 4s. 10d. for each person. The church may be visited in the summer, from 8 in the morning till 8 in the evening; and during the winter, from 11 in the morning till 3 in the afternoon. The church service is performed here twice every day, at a quarter before 10 in the morning, and at a quarter past 3; and prayers are read, &c. in the Morning Chapel, every week-day morning at 7 o'clock in the summer, and 8 in the winter, on all which occasions the Cathedral is open.'

In that same year, 1837, the Government asked through the Home Secretary, Lord John Russell, that the cathedral should be open free of charge, 'like any other national building or establishment containing works of art, historical or literary monuments, or objects of national history'. The entrance fees formed the bulk of the salaries for the staff of four virgers, whose task it was to admit the public and to maintain order. The Dean and Chapter replied that, although St Paul's had been chiefly rebuilt through parliamentary legislation and financial provision by means of the coal tax, it was no more subject to Government control than old St Paul's had been, and had not 'acquired more the character of a national building on that account'; and, moreover, it was judged necessary to charge a fee in order to set some limit on the number of casual visitors, and so to preserve decency and quiet 'in the House of God'. No extra charge was made for viewing the monuments, and 'a church ought not to be regarded in the light of a gallery of art or of a place of public exhibition'. Again, in 1842, there was pressure for free admission, after a report by a Select Committee of the House of Commons on National Monuments; and at length, in 1851, the Dean and Chapter relented and abolished the entrance fee in view of the forthcoming opening of the Great Exhibition in Hyde Park, when a record number of visitors was expected in London.

Today cathedral Chapters find themselves in a dilemma which, while similar to that of the 1840s, has its own characteristics. On the one hand the more popular cathedrals, of which St Paul's is one, are inundated with visitors (the English Tourist Board report *English Cathedrals and Tourism: Problems and Opportunities*, published in 1979, placed St Paul's in the range of 2-3 million visitors a year); and the cost of never-ending fabric repairs, exacerbated by the wear and tear of tourists' feet, is also considerable. Yet there is no Government money whatsoever for cathedrals in England and Wales, and the cost of the VAT levied on repairs is an additional burden. Visitors have very high expectations of cathedrals also in terms of sophisticated literature and presentation, a welcoming and accessible staff of clergy and virgers and administrators, and every 'event' has to be flawlessly organized and managed. The temptation to consider an admission charge is therefore both strong and understandable, either for parts of the building or even for the building as a whole. Sadly, as the English Tourist Board's research vividly demonstrated, many visitors make no voluntary contribution to St Paul's at all, perhaps imagining either that the cathedral enjoys the financial support of the State, or that it has huge resources of its own. Both assumptions are mistaken.

The question of resources brings us back to the 1830s and 1840s for, in that same period, the Government appointed an

Ecclesiastical Commission whose task it was to make substantial proposals for reforming the constitutions and finances of cathedrals. The Commission was appointed in 1835, carried out its work briskly and efficiently, and its recommendations were soon passed into legislation. The motivation behind the reforms was to appropriate the excess revenues of the richer cathedrals (which then included St Paul's) and to augment with these monies the number and the salaries of the parochial clergy, especially in the rapidly growing industrial towns and cities of the Midlands and the North of England. Nonresidentiary cathedral dignitaries, and prebendaries (except in an honorary sense), were abolished; and it was established as a norm throughout England that there should be four residentiary canons. Although St Paul's had always had four residentiaries, one of them had traditionally been the Dean; and so it was provided that there should be a fourth canonry, attached to an archdeaconry, and appointed by the Bishop of London and not the Crown.

The first holder of this new canonry was Archdeacon William Hale, appointed in 1840, who rapidly made himself indispensable in the affairs of the Chapter and instituted a reign of improvements and further reforms. The lighting and heating of the cathedral, and the management of the Fabric Fund, were amongst the matters which particularly engaged his attention. His also tackled the problem of dirt, closing the entire cathedral in the summer of 1842, and again in 1844, for vast programmes of dusting, cleaning and redecorating. The effect was apparently short-lived, as at that time the cathedral had no regular staff of cleaners.

A fresh and equally active personality appeared on the scene on 13 November 1849, with the appointment of Henry Hart Milman as Dean. Milman had previously held the Professorship of Poetry at Oxford from 1821 to 1831, a canonry of Westminster Abbey since 1835, and was a lively controversialist as a theologian.

Already, the tradition was established of holding special services in St Paul's, to mark important events or to reflect the feelings of the nation. In November 1849 there had been a Day of Thanksgiving for the cessation of the cholera epidemic; and in October 1854 a Thanksgiving Service was held for the plentiful harvest. In March 1855 there was a Day of Humiliation for the Crimean War with Russia, begun the previous year; and in May 1856, after peace had been signed, there was a

Nelson's funeral carriage reaches St Paul's.

Day of Thanksgiving. The Indian Mutiny of 1857 was similarly marked by a Day of Humiliation and, in due course, by a Thanksgiving in May 1859. On the death of Albert, the Prince Consort, in December 1861 vast crowds came to St Paul's for consolation, and Dean Milman preached an affecting sermon. By contrast, the annual service to commemorate the Great Fire of London of 1666 was finally discontinued after 1858.

Undoubtedly the most spectacular service of this time was the funeral of the Duke of Wellington on 18 November 1852. For the first time, and at Milman's suggestion, a state service was held not in the choir but beneath the dome. Contemporary illustrations show the impact of 13,000 people accommodated on tiers of temporary seating in the dome, transepts, and nave. Special lighting, incorporating a corona and gas-jets under the Whispering Gallery, was installed.

It was Milman whose imagination grasped the potential for regular worshippers of the vast unused spaces of the cathedral, first tackling the question in a memorandum of February 1850. During the following year, the year of the Great Exhibition, Evensong was held experimentally in the nave on a few occasions; and for six months a two-manual organ stood on the west gallery, to support the singing of congregations in the nave. In 1856 Tait had become Bishop of London, and had challenged the Chapters of both St Paul's and Westminster Abbey to use their vast empty spaces for regular worship. In 1858 an appeal was launched for St Paul's, the first of many subsequent appeals (the most recent being for the choral foundation in 1985); this one was for the decoration of the interior, referred to in more detail elsewhere in this book, and to provide for the accommodation of large congregations in the dome area, transepts and nave.

On Advent Sunday in November of the same year a series of services, for which 2,500 chairs were provided, began to be held under the dome. These were discontinued at Easter 1859, but revived again in suceeding years from January to Easter. In 1859 the first offertory-boxes appeared in St Paul's, to solicit funds to meet the extra costs of these special services. In 1861 the Wandsmen, still a thriving corporate body, came into existence. Their task was, and is, to supply voluntary assistance to the virgers in welcoming and showing visitors to their seats, handing out service books and papers, and generally providing for the good order and discipline of the cathedral at times of services.

Milman died in office in September 1868, and was succeeded by Dean Mansel for a short period (from December 1868 to July 1871). In August 1871 Richard William Church came from a small parish in Somerset, Whatley, to be Dean of St Paul's; and, meanwhile, in December 1868 (as we have seen earlier) Robert Gregory became a canon, and was later to be a most effective Dean. One more outstanding personality of this period was Henry Liddon, who became a canon in 1871. Dean Gregory wrote in his *Autobiography*: 'With the advent of Dr Liddon to St Paul's a new state of things commenced. His fame as a preacher was great, and so soon as it was known that he was to preach at St Paul's, a large congregation assembled. The choir would no longer find room for them; and Dr Liddon preached from the pulpit under the dome, which had been placed there for Sunday evening services that had been com- menced during the Great Exhibition of 1851. The choir was made to attend somewhat more regularly; the services were more reverent, and it was felt that a new spirit was beginning to stir in the Cathedral.'

Another crucial occasion was on 27 February 1872 when, prompted by a remark made by Canon Liddon in one of his sermons some weeks before, Queen Victoria came in solemn state to the cathedral to give thanks to God for the safe recovery of the Prince of Wales from a dangerous illness. Dean Gregory recalled that 'The Cathedral was crowded with a vast congregation, galleries having been erected wherever convenient positions for them could be found; the whole nation rang with what was being done in St Paul's, and people seemed to realise that Cathedrals might be made to fill an important position in the development of Church life'. Another memorable visit by Queen Victoria took place in 1897, when she came to give thanks for the sixty years of her reign. Two of the copes made for that occasion are on display in the cathedral Treasury.

In recent years this tradition of services to mark important anniversaries in the life of the nation has, if anything, expanded. The state funeral of Sir Winston Churchill on 30 January 1965 was an event comparable with the state funerals of Nelson and Wellington in the nineteenth century. A bronze plaque in the floor of the dome, just west of the steps leading up into the choir, records the resting place of his catafalque during the service.

On 7 June 1977 a Thanksgiving Service was held to celebrate the Silver Jubilee of the accession of Queen Elizabeth II. A special anthem was composed for the occasion by the Organist, Christopher Dearnley; Heads of State and Heads of Government from the Commonwealth were present; and every aspect of the nation's life was represented. The wedding of the Prince and Princess of Wales in July 1981 in St Paul's was again a spectacular and much appreciated success. Through such occasions a nation expresses its sense of identity, and feels the pulse of its heart. In fact, uniquely, St Paul's has three equally important roles. It is the diocesan cathedral for London, the capital city and one of the largest of all Anglican dioceses. It is a masterpiece of architecture, in a way and to a degree which never ceases to inspire those who worship in it and those who visit it. And, thirdly, it is a place where important national and international events are marked or celebrated. These three factors together give it a special place in the affections of all Christendom—and indeed those of other faiths, or none, also feel welcome in St Paul's—and it is therefore small wonder that, throughout the year but especially in the summer months, it is thronged with visitors.

In addition to the great national and international occasions there are some services which take place annually, and are important strands in the cathedral's relationships with the City of London, the Friends of the Cathedral, or with various aspects of national and Church life. For example, the Lord Mayor of London has a special relationship with St Paul's: this is marked right at the beginning of his year of office in a ceremony which takes place outside the south transept, in which he pauses in his triumphal procession through the City to be greeted by the Dean and Chapter and to be presented by them with a Bible. He also kneels for a blessing. During his year of office he will go many times to worship in St Paul's, where he has his own magnificent stall in the choir and his own vestry. The Lord Major is also ex officio a trustee of the Cathedral Trust.

Other annual occasions include the services for the Worshipful Company of Stationers, the Church Army, the Order of the British Empire, the Order of St Michael and St George, the Corporation of the Sons of the Clergy, the United Guilds, the Middlesex Regiment and, above all, the service of Thanksgiving for the Friends of St Paul's. 1986 was Industry Year, and the Queen and Prince Philip attended to hear a sermon by the Archbishop of Canterbury, Dr Robert Runcie. In it he put a special gloss on the significance of industry in the life of a nation: 'Our well-being as a nation largely depends on our manufacturing achievements. What Britain makes, makes Britain. . . . Without industry's profitable performance we should not be able to give significant help to those millions in the world who are still in thrall to poverty, illiteracy and disease.'

Responsibility for maintaining both the fabric of St Paul's and its vision rests with the Dean and Chapter, the latter consisting of the four residentiary canons. As bishop of the diocese and as Visitor to the Cathedral, the Bishop of London stands in a special relationship to the Dean and Chapter. This relationship, and all other formal aspects of their respective roles, are defined for the Dean and Chapter by the Statutes of the Cathedral, given to them by the Crown and from time to time revised. The prime responsibility of the Dean and Chapter is to maintain the cathedral for the worship of God and, in addition, the three principal roles of the cathedral—as

The Organist of St Paul's Cathedral, Mr Christopher Dearnley, at the console of the organ.

diocesan cathedral, masterpiece of architecture, and national and international religious focus—have to be kept in balance. There is a resident cathedral community in Amen Court, a few minutes' walk from the west front of St Paul's, consisting of seventeen people who work in and for St Paul's (the clergy, the Registrar, three organists, three virgers, the Secretary of the Friends, the Bookstall Manager, and the Clerk of Works). East of the cathedral is the Choir School, with five more resident members of staff and the boys of the choir. Altogether rather more than one hundred people are employed by the Dean and Chapter, and about a further one hundred and fifty work regularly for the cathedral on a voluntary basis.

The role of a cathedral can be understood in many different ways, and some will place on it different emphases from others. The worship is an indispensable part of this, for there would be no reason for a cathedral to exist if it did not sustain a community of regular worshippers some of whom, at least to some extent, are also engaged in the business of living together as a community. Linked with this commitment to unceasing worship is the relationship with the bishop and the diocese. A cathedral is so called because it is the place where the bishop's 'cathedra' or throne is located: and, although a bishop's work necessarily takes him all over his diocese, a cathedral and its Chapter surround him and support him with prayer, affection and support. In return, he supports them, and their specialist and wider ministry to the nation and the world. From time to time a bishop may hold Visitations, at which he will inquire into the effectiveness of the work of the cathedral, and into how it is nourished and maintained.

What is so striking about St Paul's is that it enshrines for so many people, both those who live in London and those who come to visit it, so much of the identity of London. It would be almost unthinkable for a visitor to come to London, hoping to catch something of its unique character as a city and to understand it a little, and yet not to pay his respects to St Paul's. By visiting it he is caught up in the continuum of its history, and of London's history; and by absorbing its atmosphere, and by participating even in a small way in the life of the cathedral, he may catch some hope for the future and for eternity.

DEANS OF ST PAUL'S SINCE THE NORMAN CONQUEST

1090	Wulfstan	1457		William Say	
1111	William	1468		Roger Radclyff	
1142	Ralph of Langford	1471		Thomas Winterbourne	
	Taurin of Stamford	1478		William Worsley	
1160	Hugh Marney	1499		Robert Sherbourn	
1181	Ralph de Diceto	1505		John Colet	
	Alard of Burnham	1519		Richard Pace	
	Gervase Hobrugg	1536		Richard Sampson	
1212	William of Basing	1540		John Innocent	
1218	Robert of Watford	1545		William May	
1228	Martin of Patshull	1553		John Feckenham	
	Walter Langford	1556		Henry Cole	
	Richard Wethershed	1559		William May	
1231	Geoffrey Lucy	1560		Alexander Nowell	
1241	William de Sancta Maria	1602		John Overall	
1243	Henry of Cornhill	1614		Valentine Carey	
1254	Walter of London	1621		John Donne	
1256	Robert Barton	1631		Thomas Winniffe	
	Peter Newport	1660		Matthew Nicholas	
1262	Richard Talbot	1661		John Barwick	
1263	Geoffrey Feringes	1664		William Sancroft	
1268	John Chishull	1677		Edward Stillingfleet	
1273	Hervey Borham	1689		John Tillotson	
1276	Thomas Inglethorp	1691		William Sherlock	
1283	Roger Lee	1707		Henry Godolphin	
1285	William de Montfort	1726		Francis Hare	
1294	Ralph Baldock	1740		Joseph Butler	
1306	Raymond de la Goth	1750		Thomas Secker	
1307	Arnold de Cantelupe	1758		John Hume	
1311	John Sandal	1766		Frederick Cornwallis	
1314	Richard Newport	1768		Thomas Newton	
1323	Vitalis de Testa	1782		Thomas Thurlow	
1323	John Everdon	1787		George Pretyman	
1336	Gilbert Brewer	1820		William van Mildert	
1353	Richard Kilmington	1826		Charles Richard Sumner	
1362	Walter Alderbury	1827		Edward Copleston	
1363	Thomas Trillek	1849		Henry Hart Milman	
1364	John Appleby	1868		Henry Longueville	
1376	Robert Brewer			Mansel	
1389	Thomas Eure	1871		Richard William Church	
1400	Thomas Stow	1891		Robert Gregory	
1406	Thomas Moor	1911		William Ralph Inge	
1421	Reginald Kentwood	1934		Walter Robert Matthews	
1441	Thomas Lisieux	1967		Martin Gloster Sullivan	
1456	Laurence Booth	1978		Alan Brunskill Webster	

BISHOPS OF LONDON AS RECORDED SINCE THE FOUNDATION OF THE DIOCESE

314	Restitutus	1280	Richard de Gravesend
		1306	Ralph de Baldock
604	Mellitus	1313	Gilbert de Seagrave
		1317	Richard de Newport
654	Cedd	1319	Stephen de Gravesend
666	Wine	1338	Richard de Bentworth
675	Erkenwald	1340	Ralph de Stratford
693	Waldhere	1355	Michael de Northburgh
706	Ingwald	1362	Simon de Sudbury
745	Ecgwulf	1375	William Courtenay
772	Sighaeh	1382	Robert Braybrooke
774	Eadberht	1405	Roger Walden
789	Eadgar	1406	Nicholas Bubwith
791	Coenwalh	1407	Richard Clifford
794	Eadbald	1421	John Kempe
794	Heathoberht	1426	William Grey
802	Osmund	1431	Robert Fitz-Hugh
811	Aethilnoth	1436	Robert Gilbert
824	Coelberht	1450	Thomas Kempe
860	Deorwulf	1489	Richard Hill
860	Swithwulf	1496	Thomas Savage
898	Heahstan	1502	William Wareham
898	Wulfsige	1504	William Barnes
926	Theodred	1506	Richard Fitz-James
953	Byrhthelm	1522	Cuthbert Tunstall
959	Dunstan	1530	John Stokesley
961	Aelfstan	1540	Edmund Bonner
996	Wulfstan	1550	Nicholas Ridley
1004	Aelfthun	1553	Edmund Bonner
1014	Aelfwig	1559	Edmund Grindal
1035	Aelfward	1570	Edwin Sandys
1044	Robert	1577	John Aylmer
1051	William the Norman	1595	Richard Fletcher
1075	Hugh de Orivalle	1597	Richard Bancroft
1085	Maurice	1604	Richard Vaughan
1108	Richard de Belmeis	1607	Thomas Ravis
1128	Gilbert	1610	George Abbot
1141	Robert de Sigillo	1611	John King
1152	Richard de Belmeis II	1621	George Montain
1163	Gilbert Foliot	1628	William Laud
1189	Richard de Ely (Fitzneal)	1633	William Juxon
1199	William de Ste-Mère -Église	1660	Gilbert Sheldon
		1663	Humfrey Henchman
1221	Eustace de Fauconberg	1675	Henry Compton
1229	Roger Niger	1714	John Robinson
1244	Fulk Basset	1723	Edmund Gibson
1260	Henry de Wingham	1748	Thomas Sherlock
1263	Henry de Sandwich	1761	Thomas Hayter
1274	John de Chishull	1762	Richard Osbaldeston

1764	Richard Terrick	1901	Arthur Foley Winnington
1777	Robert Lowth		Ingram
1787	Beilby Porteus	1939	Geoffrey Francis Fisher
1809	John Randolph	1945	John William Charles
1813	William Howley		Wand
1828	Charles James Blomfield	1956	Henry Montgomery
1856	Archibald Campbell Tait		Campbell
1869	John Jackson	1961	Robert Wright Stopford
1885	Frederick Temple	1973	Gerald Alexander Ellison
1897	Mandell Creighton	1981	Graham Douglas Leonard

LIST OF THE SURVEYORS TO THE FABRIC

Wren himself delighted to be called 'the Surveyor', and in the crypt of the Cathedral is his ceremonial measuring rod with the words 'Surveyor to the Fabric' painted on it. He and his successors include some of the most celebrated names in English architecture and English architectural history.

Period of office
1675–1723	Sir Christopher Wren
1724–1746	John James (who had been Assistant Surveyor from 1715)
1746–1756	Henry Flitcroft
1756–1766	Stiff Leadbetter
1766–1811	Robert Mylne
1811–1819	S P Cockerell
1819–1852	C R Cockerell
1852–1897	F C Penrose
1897–1906	Somers Clarke
1906–1931	Sir Mervyn Macartney
1931–1956	W Godfrey Allen
1956–1963	Lord Mottistone
1963–1969	Paul Paget
1969–1977	Sir Bernard Feilden
1978–1984	Robert Potter
1985–	Professor William Whitfield

BIBLIOGRAPHY

Like all authors I owe a tremendous debt to those who have previously explored the same paths and especially, in this context, to those who have written about the architecture and history of St Paul's or about Sir Christopher Wren. I have listed them, or anyway those to which I have most frequently had recourse, in relation to the principal sections of this book:

GENERAL

Frank Atkinson, **St Paul's and the City** (1985)
Nikolaus Pevsner and Priscilla Metcalf, **The Cathedrals of England: Southern England** (1985)

EARLY HISTORY

Bede, **A History of the English Church and People** (Translated Leo Sherley-Price 1955)
Christopher Brooke assisted by Gillian Keir **London 800–1216: the Shaping of a City** (1975)

G. H. Cook, **Old St Paul's: A Lost Glory of Medieval London** (1955)

W. Dugdale, **History of St Paul's Cathedral** (1658)

John Harvey, **English Medieval Architects: A Biographical Dictionary down to 1550** (Revised edition 1984)

William Longman, **A History of The Three Cathedrals Dedicated to St Paul in London** (1873)

John Schofield, **The Building of London** (1984)

John Stow, **Survey of London** (1598)

John Summerson, **Inigo Jones** (1966)

WREN AND THE ARCHITECTURE OF ST PAUL'S CATHEDRAL

J. A. Bennett, **The Mathematical Science of Christopher Wren** (Cambridge, 1982)

A. T. Bolton and H. D. Hendry (editors), **Wren Society** volumes (1923–43)

Howard Colvin, **A Biographical Dictionary of British Architects 1600–1840** (1978)

Kerry Downes, **The Architecture of Wren** (1982)

Kerry Downes, **Christopher Wren** (1971)

V. Fuerst, **The Architecture of Sir Christopher Wren** (1956)

Jane Lang, **Rebuilding St Paul's after the Great Fire of London** (Oxford, 1956)

Arthur F. E. Poley, **St Paul's Cathedral, London** (1932)

E. F. Sekler, **Wren and his Place in European Architecture** (1956)

John Summerson, **The Classical Language of Architecture** (revised and enlarged edition 1980)

John Summerson, **The Mind of Wren, in Heavenly Mansions and other Essays on Architecture** (1949)

Margaret Whinney, **Wren** (1971, reprinted 1985)

Christopher Wren junior, **Parentalia: or, memoirs of the family of the Wrens . . .** (1750, reprinted in facsimile 1965)

FURNISHINGS AND WORKS OF ART

David Green, **Grinling Gibbons: His Work as Carver and Statuary** (1964)

Robert Gregory, 1819–1911, **Autobiography** (1912)

Jeremy Maas, **Holman Hunt and the Light of the World** (1984)

J. Mordaunt Crook, **William Burges and the High Victorian Dream** (1981)

Victorian Church Art: catalogue of an exhibition at the Victoria & Albert Museum (1971)

MONUMENTS

Susan Beattie, **The New Sculpture** (1983)

Richard Dorment, **Alfred Gilbert** (1985)

Rupert Gunnis, **Dictionary of British Sculptors 1660–1851** (revised edition 1964)

David Irwin, **John Flaxman 1755–1826** (1979)

John Physick, **The Wellington Monument** (1970)

Benedict Read, **Victorian Sculpture** (1982)

Margaret Whinney, **Sculpture in Britain 1530–1830** (1964)

LIFE OF ST PAUL'S

George Godwin, **A History and Description of St Paul's Cathedral** (1837)

W. R. Inge, **Vale** (1934)

G. L. Prestige, **St Paul's in its Glory 1831–1911** (1955)

Annual Reports of the Friends of St Paul's

GLOSSARY

ACANTHUS Ornament based on the acanthus plant, used for the capitals of the CORINTHIAN and COMPOSITE orders.

ACROTERION/ACROTERIA (singular and plural) Miniature pedestal as placed on the three angles of a PEDIMENT in Greek CLASSICAL architecture, often elaborated with a figure or other ornament.

AEDICULE An opening (e.g. window, door, niche) framed by COLUMNS and a PEDIMENT.

AISLE A subsidiary space, separated from CHOIR, chancel, NAVE or TRANSEPT by a pierced opening (if small) or an arcade of COLUMNS and arches (if large).

ANTHEMION Originally an ornament derived from the stylized representation of a palm leaf, but also used to describe the stylized flower of the honeysuckle.

APSE The semicircular termination of part of a church, usually of the chancel or chapel at the liturgical east end.

ARCADES Arches of masonry or brickwork supported on COLUMNS or PIERS.

BALDACCHINO A canopy of honour over an altar, usually supported on four or more COLUMNS.

BALUSTRADE A low decorative wall or fence consisting of balusters, or miniature columns, supporting a top-rail.

BAROQUE The style of architecture which, emerging principally in late sixteenth-century Rome, became the dominant European style in the seventeenth and early eighteenth centuries, characterized by the use of CLASSICAL forms but given dramatic forcefulness and a strong sense of movement.

BOLECTION (moulding, ornament) An ornamental moulding convex in profile and projecting beyond the plane of the surface it frames.

BUTTRESS A vertical element of brick or masonry against or close to a wall whose purpose is to give it stability and to counteract outward thrust.

CHAPTER HOUSE A special room attached to a cathedral, collegiate or monastic church for solemn assemblies of the 'chapter' or body of priests attached to that church.

CHOIR In cathedrals, collegiate or monastic churches that part of the building east of the crossing where the daily liturgy is held.

CINQUEFOIL In GOTHIC tracery the arch at the head of a window opening or 'light' may be separated by cusps or points making three (trefoil), four (quatrefoil) or five (cinquefoil) or more divisions.

CLADDING An outer and visible cover to some element of construction.

CLASSICAL Deriving from the practice of ancient Greece or Rome.

CLERESTORY The highest level of the NAVE, above the level of the AISLE roofs, pierced with windows to provide ample light.

CLOISTER A covered walk round a courtyard or garth, usually but not always approximately square in plan, attached to a cathedral, collegiate or monastic church.

COFFER/COFFERING/COFFERED A form of decoration to ceiling or arch in which a net-like pattern of sunken panels is superimposed on the main design.

COLUMN A vertical element of brick, masonry or wood supporting an arch, beam or lintel; in CLASSICAL architecture a column consists of a base, shaft and capital all governed by special rules and relationships.

COMPOSITE One of the principal orders in CLASSICAL architecture, whose capital combines the foliated bell of the CORINTHIAN with the volutes of the IONIC order.

CONSOLE A bracket supported by a scroll or scrolls.

COPE A ceremonial vestment worn by priests and bishops, following the form of the Roman 'cappa' (a semicircular cloak with vertical bands of decoration down the front and a hood behind).

CORINTHIAN One of the principal orders in CLASSICAL architecture, the capital being an inverted bell shape and ornamented with acanthus, olive or laurel leaves.

CORNICE The uppermost of the three 'layers' of a CLASSICAL ENTABLATURE.

CROCKET A small-scale projecting ornament attached to a pinnacle or other feature in GOTHIC architecture.

CRUCIFORM Having a plan in the form of a cross.

CRYPT A chamber beneath the main floor of a church, either wholly or partially below ground level.

DECORATED The phase of GOTHIC architecture in England which lasted from c. 1290 to c. 1360.

DORIC One of the principal orders in CLASSICAL architecture, whose frieze has a rhythm of alternating TRIGLYPHS and METOPES.

ENTABLATURE The assemblage of horizontal architectural elements (architrave, frieze and cornice) supported by a column in CLASSICAL architecture.

ENTASIS A slight convex curve on the profile of a column, intended to minimize the optical illusion of a completely straight profile appearing concave.

FAÇADE The front of a building.

FIELDED PANEL A panel with a raised central area.

FLUTED Having vertical grooves, as on a COLUMN in CLASSICAL architecture.

FRIEZE The middle layer of an

ENTABLATURE, which may be plain or decoratively treated; and, by extension, any horizontal band of ornament.

GABLE The triangular-shaped area of wall at the ends of a ridge roof.

GADROONED Ornamented with a form of decoration consisting of a series of convex elements, as deployed on the font in St Paul's cathedral.

GIANT ORDER Or, alternatively, a 'colossal order': an order which extends over more than one storey of a building.

GOTHIC The style of architecture which succeeded the ROMANESQUE style (which used the round arch) *c*. 1200 in England, which used the pointed arch and continued in various phases (in England known generally as EARLY ENGLISH, DECORATED and PERPENDICULAR) until it was gradually replaced by the influence of the Renaissance.

GRAFFITO An inscription or drawing scratched on a wall or some other surface, often revealing information of very great historical interest.

GROIN VAULT An inner roof or vault in which, at its simplest, two half-round or barrel vaults intersect one another: their intersecting diagonals form 'groins'.

GUILLOCHE A pattern of interlaced spiralling shapes.

IONIC One of the principal orders in CLASSICAL architecture, identifiable by the VOLUTES in its capitals and dentils in its CORNICE.

LANCET A tall single-light window with a pointed head, occurring either singly or in groups and mostly in the context of EARLY ENGLISH GOTHIC architecture.

LITURGY A prescribed form of worship in which spoken and frequently also sung words combine with action or movement in a particular way.

LOBED Having an ear-like projection or division.

LOGGIA A covered walk pierced on one or both sides by ARCADES.

LUCARNE A small 'light' or window opening projecting from a sloping surface, e.g. of a steep roof or a spire.

LUNETTE A semi-circular window or panel.

METOPE A panel, either plain or decorated, between the TRIGLYPHS in the FRIEZE of the DORIC order.

MITRE The ceremonial headdress of a bishop, first adopted in the tenth century.

MORSE The clasp or fastening of a COPE, usually made of metal and frequently enriched with enamel or jewels.

MORTAR The binding material between stones or bricks.

MULLION In a window a mullion is a vertical member dividing the space into openings or 'lights'.

NAVE The principal or central aisle of a church, where the main congregation gathers.

OBELISK A vertical four-sided ornament, with a pyramidal top, much used in the seventeenth century.

OGIVAL In describing an arch or opening, ogival denotes a somewhat 'pinched' shape obtained by inscribing two convex arcs above and two concave arcs below.

ORDNANCE The 'ordering' of the different elements of which a building is composed.

PARAPET A low ornamental wall over a CORNICE at the top of a building (or a bridge, or gallery, or similar), sometimes solid and sometimes pierced, e.g. with balusters for decorative effect.

PEDIMENT A triangular-shaped gable over an entablature, often above a PORTICO or a door or window opening.

PERPENDICULAR The latest phase of English GOTHIC architecture, beginning in the 1330s (St Paul's chapter house being one of its earliest manifestations) and extending well into the sixteenth century.

PIER A vertical element of brick or masonry supporting an arch, beam or lintel.

PINNACLE A thin vertical ornament, rather like an attenuated pyramid, to adorn a roofline.

PLINTH The lowest projecting element of the base of a COLUMN or structure.

PORTICO At the entrance to a CLASSICAL building, a covered colonnade finished off with a BALUSTRADE or PEDIMENT.

PUTTO/PUTTI Singular and plural. Italian word denoting a playfully painted or carved or modelled representation of an angel or cupid in the form of a small naked boy.

QUADRANT A subsidiary part of a building characterized by being built on a curve which is part of a circle, a form often deployed, e.g. in a wing whose purpose is to link the main block with a lesser wing (but see also the description of the Great Model of St Paul's).

RIB VAULT An inner roof or vault in which arch-shaped ribs form a framework for the webs or infilling.

ROMANESQUE That period of English architecture following the Norman Conquest of 1066 and lasting up to c. 1200, using the round arch as opposed to the pointed arch of GOTHIC style.

RUSTICATION Treatment of masonry in which the vertical and horizontal joints are deeply gouged for monumental effect, frequently following a smaller scale than for the actual joints.

SALIENT An element or division.

SEGMENTAL Using a portion of the circumference of a circle.

SHRINE An architectural or sculptural setting for the burial place of a saint, enclosing coffin or casket.

SPANDREL The triangular area either side of the head of an arch.

SPIRELET A vertical tapering ornament, in form like a miniature spire.

STEEPLE A term which embraces the whole composition of a church tower including not only the tower itself but any spire, lantern or other elaborating feature.

TRACERY The ornamental divisions in the head of a GOTHIC window.

TRANSEPT In a cross-shaped (cruciform) church, the transverse arm of the building.

TRIGLYPH A rectangular block (one of three) alternating with METOPES in the FRIEZE of the DORIC order.

TRILOBE Having three divisions or projections, frequently ear-shaped.

TROMP L'OEIL French expression meaning, literally, 'deceive the eye', e.g. by the skilful use of one medium to represent another (as when a marbler paints a surface so skilfully that it looks very convincingly like marble).

TURRET A small subsidiary tower, often containing a stair.

TUSCAN One of the principal orders in CLASSICAL architecture, a simplified and more rustic form of the DORIC.

VENETIAN WINDOW A window with three elements, the side elements being flat-headed and the central element being taller, wider and arched.

VOLUTE An ornament shaped like a coil, used to powerful effect in BAROQUE architecture though occurring also in earlier Renaissance architecture.

ACKNOWLEDGEMENTS

I owe a special debt to the Dean and Chapter of St Paul's for so readily approving the proposal that I should write this book, and for allowing me generous access to the building. For particular help and advice I should like to express my thanks to the Dean, the Very Revd Alan Webster; the Treasurer, the Revd Canon Graham Routledge; and above all to the late Archdeacon of London, the Venerable Frank Harvey, whose untimely death in November 1986 robbed the cathedral and the City of London (not to mention the diocese of London and the Church of England at large) of a powerful advocate, a shrewd adviser, and a kindly friend who loved St Paul's single-heartedly.

At the cathedral I also owe particularly warm thanks to Commander Charles Shears OBE, the Registrar and Receiver General; to Dixon Asquith, the Head Virger, and his colleagues who bear the brunt of the tremendous pressure of visitors to St Paul's and who are, as it were, at the sharp edge of its care and conservation; to Dr Frank Atkinson, Librarian; Selene Mills, former Assistant Librarian; the late Robert Harvey, Clerk of the Works; and the Surveyor of the Fabric, Professor William Whitfield CBE.

A number of friends and colleagues have read different sections of the book in draft, or have made helpful suggestions and comments, and I would like to express my warmest thanks to them all and especially to Professor Lady Wedgwood, Dr Richard Gem, John Schofield, Stephen Dykes Bower, Sir Bernard Feilden CBE, Robert Crayford, Robert Potter, Roy Rushton (who was Deputy Surveyor from 1965 to 1969), Anthony New, Brian Thomas OBE, Dr John Physick CBE, John Skelton, David Kindersley, David Peace MBE, Piers Rogers (Secretary of the Royal Academy of Arts) and Constance-Anne Parker (Archivist to the Royal Academy of Arts). If, in spite of all their help and encouragement, errors of fact or judgment have crept in then the fault is entirely my own.

The photography for this book has always been envisaged as a proper complement to the text. No-one could have taken more trouble, or been a more supportive partner, than Malcolm Crowthers. I would like to thank the Librarian of Worcester College, Oxford, and the Librarian of All Souls College, Oxford, for providing facilities for the photography of drawings in their care; and to the governing bodies of those colleges for allowing them to be reproduced. Thanks to the Guildhall Library for permission to reproduce the plan on p. 70. Connie Austen Smith deserves special thanks as the originator of the series, following a suggestion I made; and Barbara Fuller deserves no less for being a stalwart editor.

I want to thank Susan Neve, Joan Denne and Roy Grant for their help in the preparation of the text, and for much practical assistance and encouragement; and, finally, I should have been unable to undertake the work at all without the unflagging support of Dana Josephson who also gave me invaluable advice of an editorial kind. To him, therefore, the book is dedicated—with gratitude and affection.

INDEX

Numeral in *italics* refer to captions, numerals in brackets, e.g. (25), indicate the
number of monument or memorial in Chapter Six, and (L) indicates ledgers.